Leonard Osborn

"Dauntless he ..."

by

Tony Joseph

Bunthorne Books

Bristol

2007

"Leonard Meryll, Leonard Meryll,
Dauntless he in time of peril ..."
                    (The Yeomen of the Guard)

D'Oyly Carte Personalities Series

1: Frederick Neebe
2: Charles Goulding
3: Aileen Davies
4: Evelyn Gardiner
5: Emmie Owen and Florence Perry
6: Leonard Osborn

© Tony Joseph 2007

ISBN: 978-0-9507992-8-5

Published by:
Bunthorne Books
55 Brynland Avenue
Bristol
BS7 9DX

Printed by:
4word Ltd
Unit 15
Baker's Park
Cater Road
Bristol
BS13 7TT

Contents

Leonard Osborn as a young man
(Melvyn Tarran collection)

Introduction

Why Leonard Osborn?

For anyone who wants to write a biography of a member, or members, of the D'Oyly Carte Opera Company there is no shortage of potential subjects. There are at the very least two thousand five hundred people to choose from; and since records of the personnel of the Company's early years are some way from complete, two thousand five hundred may be a considerable underestimate. We are, after all, talking about a Company that was in existence for more than a hundred years.

So which of those two thousand five hundred people do you go for? To D'Oyly Carte followers, all of them are or were by definition special. Every one of them as likely as not would have held you fascinated if you'd asked them to dinner; so fascinated, indeed, that you might have asked them to stay on for the weekend. And this being so, you might as well drop all their names into a hat and settle the identity of your subject by pulling out a name at random.

Well, you *might*. But of course that wouldn't really do. Why? Let's put it like this. Even accepting that all D'Oyly Carte people were special, there will have been for each of us – there must have been – some who were not just special but *very* special. No one except a saint can love two and a half thousand people equally – that's not the way things happen. Therefore it's almost certainly from the list of those *very special* people that you'll find your subject will eventually emerge.

And it's not only a near certainty that this will be so. It's also vital. Because once you've chosen your subject, what in effect you'll be doing is inviting that person to stay with you – to live with you – not merely for a weekend, not even for a week or a fortnight, but for months if not years as you work your way through the whole researching and writing process; and you wouldn't want just anybody – would you? – to stay as long as that. That's why it matters more than anything that he or she is someone who never ceases to fascinate you, someone whose company you never cease to relish, someone with whom you can empathise, someone whose difficult side you can accept with understanding, someone you care about deeply.

And that, in a nutshell, is why I've chosen Leonard Osborn. Leonard Osborn fulfils all these criteria. Leonard Osborn is one of my all-time D'Oyly Carte favourites.

Leonard Osborn's D'Oyly Carte career spanned no fewer than forty-three years (1937-1980) and fell into three distinct phases. From 1937 to 1940 he was a chorister and small-part player. Then in 1946, after a gap necessitated by war service in the RAF, he was promoted to principal tenor, and remained a principal tenor till 1959. Finally, after another, much longer gap he went back between 1977 and 1980 for a spell as the Company's Director of Productions.

His overall reputation, though, was largely based on his years as a principal tenor. In that capacity he was enormously popular, and I don't think it's exaggerating to say that, with the possible exception of Derek Oldham in the 1920s and '30s, he was the most popular tenor the Company ever had. Here are the feelings about him of just three D'Oyly Carte enthusiasts from down the years:

> "I have very pleasurable memories of Osborn. In general terms he was an excellent G&S tenor."
>
> (Geoffrey Dixon)
>
> "I have often cited Leonard Osborn as being one of the finest G&S tenors of all time."
>
> (Chris Webster)
>
> "I feel privileged to have met Leonard Osborn on many occasions. As well as being a consummate artist he was a genuinely charming man; qualities not often found together in the same person."
>
> (Tony Gower)

All of which suggests that in calling him one of my D'Oyly Carte favourites I am not alone.

In consequence, his huge popularity is an essential part of his story. And had his reputation rested on his stage performances alone, it would have been totally secure and unchallengeable. But unfortunately for the way he is regarded today, two other aspects of his D'Oyly Carte career come into the picture and he emerges from these nothing like so happily.

There was, on the one hand, his spell as Director of Productions which, while it scarcely dented his image with the D'Oyly Carte audiences, did little for the way he was seen within the Company itself. In terms of his reputation as a whole, though, this phase can now be largely discounted. But it's a different matter when it comes to the other aspect: his recordings.

Between 1949 and 1955 Leonard Osborn featured in no fewer than ten of the eleven D'Oyly Carte recordings issued during those years, and I'm going to stick my neck out straight away and say that, in my opinion, even his best recordings don't really do him justice. It's not that I can't enjoy them for what they are – recordings. It's simply that I'm convinced that to get the full impact and dynamism of his performances you needed to see him in person on stage. Nor is this just my opinion. It seems – which is encouraging - to be the opinion of *most* people who saw him.

But none of that counts for even five minutes with any number of people who have come along since – people who know him from his recordings alone – and this is where the less than happy side of the picture enters into things. These people find it hard to credit that he made an impact at all, never mind one that could conceivably be called dynamic by anybody. More even than that, they react to his recordings with downright hostility. On this count it's worth quoting part of an email about him that I received from a G&S fan in Australia, Bruce Doery:

> "It seems that to make disparaging remarks about Leonard Osborn is nowadays the in-thing. Should anyone mention him on [the G&S website] SavoyNet, particularly in a favourable way, it is almost certain to bring a number of negative comments.
>
> A little while ago, a fairly new contributor implied she preferred his more robust tenor voice to that of [his best known contemporary D'Oyly Carte tenor] Tom Round, and she almost brought the wrath of the gods upon her.
>
> Recently somebody mentioned a photograph in which he was smoking a cigarette, to which several people responded by saying that this might help explain the rather unpleasant sounds that he made."

So that's an essential part of his story too.

Deciding you'd like to research and write a biography of such-and-such a person, though, doesn't mean you automatically go ahead and do it just like that. For no matter who you want to write about, it won't be long before you find you need to check the reaction of certain *other* people to the idea. It may turn out, for example, that some crucial material relating to your subject is unavailable to you, because the individuals or institutions that hold that material won't let you look at it – or even if they let you look at it, won't let you quote from it. So what do you do then? Go ahead with the biography regardless? Or accept you've been given a brush-off and simply abandon it?

The attitude of other people is particularly important if any of those people are your subject's descendants. Would you go ahead if those descendants, or any of your subject's other living relatives, were hostile to the idea of the biography or even merely unenthusiastic about it? Some biographers may possibly do so – may actually regard such hostility or lack of enthusiasm as a challenge.

But I wouldn't do so myself – not even for an hundred crowns and wine with my dinner to boot. I write because I enjoy writing; and I wouldn't enjoy any writing project if I felt there was a person or people in the background chuntering on about "these bloody authors" and "their wretched scribblings" (or whatever) all the time I was engaged on it.

However, going by my own experience I'd say that brush-offs are rare. In two or three instances I've had to overcome some initial – and entirely understandable – suspicion; in each case I came into the lives of those concerned as a total stranger about whom they knew nothing. But including Leonard Osborn I've now written biographies of eight D'Oyly Carte people. And overall I've found the current descendants of my chosen subjects full of encouragement and eager to help in any way they can.

I found this indeed right from the first, with my biography of George Grossmith, the man who created most of the G&S patter roles. No fewer than four members of the Grossmith family allowed me to see and quote from letters, papers, press cuttings and other relevant material in their possession, as well as showing continuing interest in the whole project. When I contemplated doing Charles Goulding, one of the tenors of the interwar years, I received strong encouragement from Goulding's son Peter. When I followed this with a life of Aileen Davies, a soubrette of the same period, I received equal encouragement from *her* son David. And now, with Leonard Osborn, I've received the same encouragement from *his* son Tony and, through Tony, his other son Martin and other members of the Osborn family.

When I first contacted Tony Osborn, he wrote in reply that he'd be pleased to answer any questions about his father that I might ask; and he has done so readily on any number of occasions, even when the subject matter of those questions was less than comfortable. He also read parts of this book in draft form, and I am immensely grateful to him in every respect. Without his help I would, through ignorance, have omitted another essential part of Leonard Osborn's story, the vicissitudes of his private life.

A second person I want particularly to thank is Tony Gower. Tony Gower and I first met in the mid-1950s when we were more or less (as Leonard Osborn put it every time he played Earl Tolloller) "boys together", and we share a wealth of memories from those days. Tony, as the quote on page 2 will have indicated, was always as great a fan of Leonard Osborn as I was myself. It was he who first suggested him as a subject for this series of biographies; and it was he who, when I was ready to start, put me in touch with Tony Osborn. During the months I was working on the book I discussed all sorts of points with him, and he too read it in draft. He also helped prepare the illustrations. His encouragement and support have been invaluable.

Other people I'd like to thank for their encouragement and help are Katie Barnes, Reg and Janet Brown, Diana Burleigh, Michael Butler, Alison Cooper, Graham Copeland, Geoffrey Dixon, Bruce Doery, Peter Downes, Jon Ellison and Joy Mornay, Mary Gilhooly, Roger Goodwin, Bruce Graham, Neville Griffiths and Elizabeth Howarth, Janet and Geoff Guppy, Kevin Hewitt, Trevor Hills, Patricia Leonard, David Mackie, Marcia Menter, Roderick Murray, Peter Parker, Jean Pratt, Frederick Sinden and Beryl Dixon, Jeffrey Skitch, Kenneth Snowdin, Melvyn Tarran, Ernie and Vicky Thomas, Michael Walters and Rob Weston.

Permission to reproduce letters, photographs and other material relating to Leonard Osborn is given by the D'Oyly Carte Opera Trust Ltd. Copyright is protected and these materials may not be reproduced in any medium without permission of the D'Oyly Carte Opera Trust Ltd.

All the letters (except that on page 53) reproduced or referred to in this book are in the D'Oyly Carte Opera Company Archive. The Archive also holds the files of audition and Company records.

I am particularly grateful to George Low for information he obtained from the Company pay sheets, formerly held in the Savoy Theatre; and I should also particularly like to thank Barry Pendry, a graphologist, for permission to quote from a character analysis of Leonard Osborn he provided for me, first mentioned on page 9.

The photographs taken by Houston Rogers are reproduced by permission of the Theatre Museum, V&A.

Finally I should like to thank Gordon Young, John Roost, Steve Drew and Dave Vinson of *4word Ltd*, my printers, for all their help in bringing this book to fruition; and Joy, for cheerfully coping with one of the drawbacks of self-publishing: living in a house in which books seem permanently to be tumbling through every crack in the walls.

Tony Joseph

There's just one other point here. The period when Leonard Osborn was a D'Oyly Carte performer was still a time when men were routinely referred to by their surnames, and I realised when I started on this book that I needed to decide how I was going to refer to him myself. In my own mind I'd always thought of him simply as "Leonard"; and when, without prompting, a number of people I contacted at this time simply referred to him as "Leonard" too, that settled it. "Leonard" he would be.

And with that, it's time to start on his story itself. Or to put it in the words of another line he spoke each time he played Tolloller:

"And now, my lords" (should any lords be reading this) "to the business of the day."

"He's Good, Isn't He?", 1914-39

It was Saturday June 4th 1949. The D'Oyly Carte Opera Company was in the third week of a six week London season at Sadler's Wells. Among the audience that afternoon or evening were my father and myself. I was then eleven years old, and it was the fourth D'Oyly Carte performance to which he'd taken me. The previous three had been *The Mikado*, *Patience* in 1947 and, in 1948, *Cox and Box* and *HMS Pinafore*. So which was the opera being performed this time? The answer was *Ruddigore*.

It was the first time *Ruddigore* had been played in London for nine years. *Ruddigore* was among the operas the costumes and scenery for which had been destroyed by an enemy bomb during the war. It had now been given new costumes and sets, and to mark its London reappearance it had also been played on the season's first three nights.

I don't imagine I was the only eleven year old in the audience the performance we were there. But equally I can't believe any of the others outdid me in the excitement they were feeling as we waited for the house lights to go down and the performance to begin. *Ruddigore* was one of only three of the operas of which we had the full set of records at home, so I knew all the music and words of the songs in advance, which had not been the case with two of the three operas I'd seen previously, and which made the sense of anticipation all the greater.

Already I'd seized on the programme – seized on it the moment we were in our seats. The programme was a typical Sadler's Wells programme of the decade, small and compact – so small and compact, indeed, it could fit easily and unfolded in your pocket. It had a cover of pillar-box red, and advertised such things as Gilbey's Gin, McFarlane Lang's "British Biscuits at their Best" and "Lip Line: a new lipstick technique". But I wasn't interested in the adverts, not even the one for the biscuits. What I wanted was to find out details of the actual performance and, in particular, to study the cast list – who was playing which part. Even at eleven years old this totally fascinated me.

Certainly there wasn't any doubt in my mind who came top of the list, even though in the programme his name came last – last, that is, among the men: Darrell Fancourt, who was down to play Sir Roderic Murgatroyd, just as he was

Sir Roderic on our records. He'd been in each of the operas I'd seen previously, and his performance was going to be – wasn't it? – the highlight of *Ruddigore* just as it had previously been the highlight of *Patience*, *Pinafore* and, of course, *The Mikado*. Other names on that cast list included Ella Halman, another particular favourite (Dame Hannah); Martyn Green (Robin Oakapple); Richard Watson (Sir Despard); Radley Flynn (Old Adam); Margaret Mitchell (Rose Maybud); and Pauline Howard (Mad Margaret).

And the performance itself, once it got under way … did it live up to my expectations? I can answer that question without hesitation. It lived up to them to such an extent that by the time the final curtain came down I knew with complete certainty that, of all the G&S operas, even those I hadn't yet seen or fully heard, *Ruddigore* was my favourite – and my favourite it has remained to this day.

But despite my total absorption, my total delight, in everything that made up that performance, there was one aspect of it that stood out – stood out with no argument – as the top delight of all: the scenes featuring not Sir Roderic but the one main character I haven't yet mentioned: Richard (Dick) Dauntless.

And this was a surprise. This was something I hadn't expected at all. On our records Dick Dauntless was sung by Derek Oldham, and Derek Oldham's performance on those records had never done anything for me whatsoever. But in that performance at Sadler's Wells, Dick Dauntless was played by Leonard Osborn.

We'd seen Leonard Osborn twice previously, Dad and I, first as the Duke of Dunstable in *Patience* and then as Box in *Cox and Box*. We'd liked him in both parts, and on one of those occasions I'd got his autograph. But his Dick Dauntless was something else again. The sheer dash, the sheer vitality of his portrayal, the charisma (not that I knew the word charisma at the time), the exuberance of his first entrance, his opening song, his dialogue – and above all his hornpipe, given once then rapturously encored. Never was an encore more eagerly demanded. Never was one more heartily deserved. Even though he had relatively little to do in Act Two, he made Dick Dauntless the most important character in the show.

Afterwards, in the warmth of that summer day, Dad and I stood among the fans who hovered near the stage door, and we (or at least Dad) managed to speak briefly to two or three members of the Company as they emerged. Curiously I don't remember Leonard on this occasion being among them. But one person we definitely spoke to was Robert (Bob) Hugh Jones, the Company's Business Manager; and in the course of the conversation Dad mentioned Leonard Osborn and how impressed with him we'd been.

Jones smiled and nodded in agreement.

"Yes," he said. "He's good, isn't he?"

Leonard Alfred George Osborn came into the world on November 11th 1914 at 20 Gilbey Road, Tooting, in South–West London, the youngest of four children of Frederick Robert Osborn, a journeyman baker, and his wife Louisa Emily, born Louisa Earl.

Leonard's birthplace in Tooting, as it is today
(Photograph: Bruce Graham)

In choosing what to call their four children the two of them went, sensibly enough, for names that were popular at the time: Frederick (junior) the eldest, Phyllis, Mabel and Leonard. But for anyone with a knowledge of Gilbert and Sullivan those four names have a particular resonance. All are names of G&S characters, with Frederic and Mabel actually the names of the two young lovers in *The Pirates of Penzance* – which is an interesting coincidence, even if nothing more.

Anyone born in November 1914 was, by definition, a First World War baby, even though the war had then been in progress less than four months. Frederick Osborn duly fought in that war, almost certainly as a volunteer, but at least he avoided the trenches. Instead he spent four or five years in Egypt, the main British base for land operations against a forgotten enemy of that time, Turkey.

But at length the war came to an end and in due course the world moved into the 1920s and '30s. Simultaneously Leonard himself moved through babyhood, childhood and, eventually, adolescence. Were childhood and adolescence happy times for him? Taken all in all, and though he was indulged and sometimes spoilt by his older siblings, it seems doubtful, for the atmosphere at home was hardly relaxed.

Partly this was due to Frederick Osborn. Having come back from Egypt he was frequently out of work, and when he had work, and consequently a certain amount of money, he would fritter that money away all too quickly. But it was still more to do with Louisa. Frederick was the silent, anything-for-a-quiet-life type. Louisa was not. Necessity had forced her to become the family's main breadwinner, and this saw her spending long hours ironing in a laundry while struggling to bring up the four children and ruling the roost, a domestic tyrant, at home. In the grim words of one family member who was around at that time, she was nothing less than "a cruel Victorian", a "very very strict" disciplinarian who was never slow to dish out punishment to her offspring for misbehaviour.

Kenneth Snowdin, son of Mabel, recounts a family story of her reaction on one occasion when the misbehaving culprit was Leonard. He (Leonard) had developed the habit of loudly saying "Ouch!" as though he'd been hit when one of his siblings was somewhere nearby, the result being that whichever of the latter it was "got a whack" for apparently hurting him. One day when he tried this on, however, she spotted what he was up to, and promptly

"caught him by the scruff of the neck, and led him down the long hall and out to the front steps saying 'I'll give you *ouch*, my boy,' all the while either whacking or kicking his backside. That was a trick he never tried again."

So clearly her methods of punishment worked. But what effect did they have on him? During the course of researching his life I asked Barry Pendry, a graphologist, to do a character analysis of Leonard as revealed by his

Frederick and Louisa Osborn with their four children: Frederick, Mabel,
Phyllis – and Leonard, the little boy sitting at the front

handwriting on one of his letters. And though knowing nothing about Leonard in advance, Pendry latched on to this aspect of his upbringing straight away:

"At first sight of the letter one could be forgiven for thinking that it had come from a female hand, i.e. an older female, which leads me to think that his early life was heavily influenced by the precepts and tendencies of a grandmother or similar role model, with strong ideas of right and wrong, coupled with strict morals and a good degree of caution."

Substitute his mother for "a grandmother" as role model, and there you have it.

But if he was given little or no opportunity to shine and be himself at home, it was a different matter when it came to his schooling. He was a bright boy, quick to learn. Possibly because of his background and the fact that, as Kenneth Snowdin puts it, "the family would not be able to fund all the extras", he was rejected by two prestigious public schools, Christ's Hospital (Bluecoat) School and Merchant Taylors'. But that, as it turned out, was not a permanent setback, for in 1928, at the age of thirteen, he won a scholarship to the Bec School in Tooting.

It was the best thing that could have happened to him. He and the school suited each other to perfection – so much so that when, six years later, a few months before he left, his headmaster wrote a testimonial for him so effusive that to describe it as glowing would be a positive understatement. That testimonial, which is self-explanatory, is worth quoting in full:

"I can strongly recommend L.A.G. Osborn for favourable consideration by the Kitchener Scholarship Selection Committee.

His application form will clearly reveal the circumstances of his parents, including the unemployment of his father, an ex-serviceman with overseas service.

I am more concerned in this testimonial with the boy's character and attainments. In spite of all difficulties and financial hardships (which were concealed in a spirit of defensible pride from myself and my colleagues) the boy has won his way most successfully up the school to the Upper Sixth. He has shown determination and grit throughout, and has firmly established a very high reputation. He has taken every advantage of his opportunities, both in work and in school games and activities. Coming rather late to us, he obtained his General School Certificate (and Matriculation) at his first attempt in 1932, with two Distinctions and four Credits, and we expect him to do very well indeed in the Higher Certificate Examination (and Intermediate) next June. If he is given the opportunity of a university career, I can confidently predict a high Honours Degree in Science.

His all-round development has been the most gratifying feature about him. He has made his mark in Games (full colours in rugby and athletics); in House Affairs (house rugby and athletics captains); in School Affairs (a school monitor); and in Dramatics and Music. It should be remarked that he has had leading parts in school plays for the last two or three years, and that he promises well as a singer.

Yet he has remained unspoilt, always anxious to do still better, and invariably unselfish in his attitude towards school affairs. He exercises an excellent influence, particularly over younger boys, whom he controls with tact and consideration.

I know of no other boy who has so successfully overcome his difficulties and hardships, and I therefore recommend him most strongly for a Kitchener Scholarship."

But now comes a puzzle. Did he, with or without a Kitchener Scholarship, go on to university and get that expected degree? There are pointers both ways. The most significant pointer suggesting that he did get a degree comes on a form which he filled up sometime in the mid-1950s. This was a form distributed by the D'Oyly Carte office asking members of the Company at that time for biographical information that could be used, if required, for publicity purposes; and on it Leonard wrote that he held a B.Sc. It's there – in his own handwriting. And it's something that in D'Oyly Carte circles was quite widely believed. Isn't all this proof enough?

Strangely, no. For against that, Tony Osborn and other members of the family are convinced of the opposite: that he *never* got a degree. And certainly if he did go to university, I've been unable to find out which one. Moreover there's the fact that a degree course, particularly one in science, would have lasted at least three years, and it's almost impossible to see when he could have fitted it in, given what were to be all his other activities at the relevant time.

So if he didn't go to university, what did he do instead? For a brief period, it seems, he started to train to become a schoolmaster. But fairly soon, or maybe even simultaneously, he had to start job hunting, not a prospect to relish in the 1930s as the unemployment of his father would have made clear; and this was so even though the Depression which had engulfed the country – and the world – a few years before was, however slowly, beginning to lift. And indeed the job he eventually obtained was not in a school but in industry. For, possibly helped by a family connection, he was taken on as an analytical chemist in a silk-printing mill at Hackbridge near Sutton in Surrey for a wage of three pounds ten shillings a week.

Meanwhile in his spare time he had continued acting and singing. As a youngster he had been a boy soprano; and it was as a boy soprano that he'd had his first experience of Gilbert and Sullivan. "I remember in rehearsals [for school concerts] singing Mabel in *The Pirates of Penzance* and Josephine in *HMS Pinafore*," he told an interviewer many years later, though at the actual performances the parts were sung by two of the teachers' wives. "But I sang 'Pretty Polly Oliver' [and] I still remember what the school paper said: 'Master Leonard Osborn sang Pretty Polly Oliver with all the delicate trill of a girl of fourteen.' You can imagine what I went through until the end of term."

Then, after his voice broke and during his period as a chemist, he sang in the choir of St James's Church in Piccadilly, "a very fashionable church", and St Botolph's in the City. For his efforts at these two venues he earned, respectively, twenty and twenty-five guineas a year, and with this money he paid for singing lessons with a man named Frederick Field-Hyde.

He also at some point joined an amateur operatic society and possibly an amateur dramatic society too. The operatic society was one which, he later claimed, "wanted men" (not that, for an amateur society, there was anything unusual about that) and in due course he was cast in principal roles in three productions: *The Rebel Maid*, *Merrie England* - and *The Mikado*, in which he played Nanki-Poo. And this led on to what effectively became the main interest and motivating force of his life: G&S.

In the audience at one performance of *Merrie England* was Leonard Rooke, the Advance Publicity Manager of the D'Oyly Carte Opera Company. He (Rooke) was obviously impressed by Leonard's showing. He suggested to him that he apply to D'Oyly Carte for an audition, and may even have personally recommended him. It was the autumn of 1937. Leonard was then coming up to twenty-three. He was not really happy working as a chemist. He doubted whether his long-term prospects in that line added up to much either. "I found that degrees in science were at a discount in industry," he wrote on that previously mentioned D'Oyly Carte form; and either immediately or before very long he took up Rooke's suggestion.

A date for an audition was fixed: Thursday October 28th. It was held in the Savoy Theatre. At that audition he sang a setting of Shakespeare's "O Mistress Mine". It worked. He was immediately given the nod and taken on by the Company as a tenor chorister and understudy, with a weekly salary of four pounds, which was then the D'Oyly Carte chorister's standard rate.

On his audition record it was noted that his voice quality was "G" (for "good"), that he had a "real tenor voice", a vocal range from A to B flat and that his dialogue, too, was "good". Whoever made those notes, though, misspelt his surname, adding an *e* on the end, so that he went down in the file as "Leonard Osborne", a common misspelling of the family name that he'd probably got used to even before he was out of short trousers.

Following the audition came a final week at the printing mill while he worked his notice. Then it was back to the Savoy for the start of his D'Oyly Carte career, which took the form of a fortnight's sessions with "Miss Evans". "Miss Evans" was Maud Evans, the Company's long established repetiteur. Her job was to take new choristers through all their music, and she did this with a formidable no-nonsense thoroughness. By the end of that fortnight Leonard, working both with her and on his own for something like seven hours a day, had duly learned the chorus music of every opera then in the D'Oyly Carte repertoire. And his efforts in this respect did not go unnoticed. It was entered on his Company record card that he was, as the phrase went, a "very quick study". Then he was off to join the Company itself for his first performances on stage.

The D'Oyly Carte Company in those years of unemployment and economic depression was a Company of enviable stability. If the 1930s weren't quite its Golden Age or decade in the way the 1920s had been – a decade in which its vigour and brilliance were generally considered to have been unsurpassed – it still had enormous prestige. "The artists love their work, and it is surely common knowledge that young singers are anxious to get into the Gilbert and Sullivan operas, and that, when they do, they remain with the Company for many years," as its current head, Rupert D'Oyly Carte, was to put it in a letter to *The Times* in 1938. While among its leading performers there was still a full array of talent.

Top of the list in this respect was Martyn Green. After years of understudying and playing second fiddle to Henry Lytton, Martyn Green had finally taken over from Lytton as principal comedian and leader of the Company in 1934. And if he was never quite to achieve the godlike status that Lytton had achieved (to have done so would have been to achieve the virtually impossible) he had quickly succeeded in establishing himself in his own right to an extent that only a performer of immense virtuosity could have managed.

Something of the same could be said of Sydney Granville who, six years earlier, had replaced the effervescent and hugely lovable Leo Sheffield in the heavy baritone "Pooh-Bah" roles; while in the case of Darrell Fancourt there was no need to mention any other name at all, as he (Fancourt) had been one of the standard-bearers of the Golden Age himself, having played the bass "Mikado" roles ever since 1920. Two other stalwarts of the 1930s were Leslie Rands, who played the light baritone roles, and Marjorie Eyre, the principal soubrette; and yet another figure present throughout the decade was John Dean, the senior principal tenor. By contrast, the other principal tenor, John Dudley, had joined the Company only a few months before Leonard. But even so, he'd hardly been slow to make his mark.

Nor were the talents of many of the choristers to be underestimated. Moreover, as Rupert D'Oyly Carte had indicated, they boasted among their number a fair few long-stayers too; and into the solid ranks of this Company Leonard felt he fitted right from the start. As he explained some years afterwards: "I found myself earning four pounds a week for doing what I enjoyed instead of three pounds ten shillings for what I didn't."

The Company when he joined them were about to start the second week of a three week season in Edinburgh, and this was followed by seasons in Aberdeen and Glasgow which took things well into the New Year, 1938. Then, moving south, they played seven venues around England before, on May 30th, opening a seven week central London season at the Scala Theatre in Charlotte Street. Up to that point Leonard seems to have gone on at every performance as a chorister pure and simple. Now at certain performances at the Scala, however, he was asked for the first time to play a couple of small parts.

This would have been significant for any promising chorister. But for a tenor it was *especially* significant, as there's a distinct lack of small parts for the G&S tenor to play. Compared with the basses and baritones, for whom there are any number of such parts – "spit and cough parts" as they were called - the tenors have just three: Leonard Meryll and First Yeoman in *The Yeomen of the Guard* and Francesco in *The Gondoliers*; and the last of these, with just one solo couplet to sing, can scarcely be called a "part" at all.

True there can be added another five – the Headsman and the two Citizens in *Yeomen*, the Solicitor in *Patience* and the Associate in *Trial by Jury* – that require no solo singing and which, accordingly, a male chorister of any voice can play. True, too, there is *Trial by Jury's* tenor lead – the Defendant – to be taken into account, along with the tenor role of Box in *Cox and Box*, the other curtain-raiser the Company used. But as though to re-emphasise the tenor choristers' lack of opportunities, these two parts were quite often given to one or other of the tenor principals, and the same applied to Leonard Meryll. So when at the Scala Leonard on different occasions played the two *Yeomen* parts – Leonard Meryll and First Yeoman – it could be seen as a genuine step up.

In addition during these first months he learned and was rehearsed in the principal roles he'd been put down to understudy – though how many roles this amounted to and which roles they were is impossible to say, as with one exception (see page 19) he was never called upon to play any of them in actual performance. According to the report of a talk he gave to the Gilbert and Sullivan Society nineteen years later, he studied the tenor parts from the wings, "particularly Hilarion" in *Princess Ida*, then being played by John Dudley – which is worth noting as much as anything for the fact that Hilarion was one of only three principal tenor roles in the pre-war repertoire that he was never to play on stage.

But whichever the roles were, he was trained in them – taught how to play them the D'Oyly Carte way – by the Company's longstanding Stage Director (as he was called) the legendary J.M. Gordon, who had learned the art of stage technique by studying and absorbing the technique of Gilbert himself. He (Leonard) was taught how to deliver the dialogue; how to say every line. He was taught characterisation, had it meticulously explained to him what was required in every part he might play. He was drilled with minute precision in every move he had to make every second he was on the stage. Nothing in Gordon's world was left to chance.

The Scala season ended on July 16th, and the Company broke up for their annual vacation. They came together again – or, rather, the chorus members came together again – not immediately to perform on stage but, along with Martyn Green, Sydney Granville and three D'Oyly Carte figures from the past as well as a number of outsiders, to film *The Mikado*. The filming took place at Pinewood Studios in Buckinghamshire, and Leonard duly went on to celluloid as a Japanese guard. It was a novel experience for most, if not all, those involved. It was also the first time any of the G&S operas had been given cinematic treatment.

The new D'Oyly Carte season proper began in Bristol on September 12th, and the next few weeks saw Leonard playing several performances not only as Leonard Meryll or First Yeoman but as the Defendant and Francesco too, sharing the first three of these parts with another tenor chorister, Thomas Hancock. Of the four parts the Defendant is really the only one that gives the performer the chance to make any significant impact, and sure enough he got mentioned for his performances in the role in a number of newspaper reviews.

Leonard as the Defendant, 1939
(Photograph: The *Sphere*)

For example: "Leonard Osborne [*sic*] sang well as the Defendant," wrote one reviewer when the Company played *Trial by Jury* in Nottingham. "Leonard Osborn played the Defendant in excellent voice," wrote another when they were in Norwich.

The same was true in the New Year, 1939, by which time they had embarked on a five month tour of America, the third such D'Oyly Carte tour of the decade. They started the tour in New York, and actually cast off with *Trial by Jury* as curtain-raiser to *The Pirates of Penzance*. "Leonard Osborn makes a handsome if somewhat colourless Defendant," wrote the critic from the *New York Post*, one of the most surprising notices Leonard ever received anywhere; "colourless" is the last thing he was. And another less than fulsome notice of his performance in the part appeared in the Washington *Evening Star* some weeks later:

> "Leonard Osborn, whose face looked new, but we may be wrong, lent a tenor voice to the role of the Defendant which somehow had a hard time climbing over the orchestra into the first rows, but may have been better farther back."

Returning to England in May, the Company played another London season, this time at Sadler's Wells, then in mid-July they broke up once again for their annual vacation.

Leonard among the chorus of Peers in *Iolanthe*, 1939
(Photograph: The *Sphere*)

Flight-Lieutenant, 1939-46

Leonard had now been in the Company well over eighteen months; months of what today would be called job satisfaction and personal fulfilment. He had, it seemed, settled on his career; and there was every indication, those American critics notwithstanding, that he would do well in it. That is, given normal times.

But those eighteen months and more could hardly be considered normal times. Those eighteen months were months in which Britain and Europe teetered on the brink of another war; months that included the Munich Crisis and Hitler's taking over of both Austria and Czechoslovakia. The threat of war, though there were periods when it appeared to recede, was present in the background throughout. And in late August, by which time the Company had re-convened for the start of their next tour, international tension had increased to such an extent that it seemed almost certain that something would snap at any moment.

The tour opened on August 28th with a week in Bournemouth. A newspaper reporter described the atmosphere. Many local people that week, he wrote, would be finding "an antidote to pressing anxieties and preoccupations in the joys of Savoy Opera"; and the performances that were booked made up a typical D'Oyly Carte bill, from *The Mikado* on the Monday to two performances of *The Gondoliers* on the Saturday. During the second of those performances the theatre was lashed by torrential rain which flooded all the ground floor dressing rooms. Meanwhile the previous day Hitler had invaded Poland and, with that, the long-feared European war became reality.

On the Sunday, September 3rd, the Company moved along the coast from Bournemouth to Southsea, where they were booked to open the day after. But that same Sunday Neville Chamberlain, the Prime Minister, announced Britain's entry into the war – and suddenly, for G&S as for everything else, the world was a different place. Among other measures, the Government announced the closing of all theatres with immediate effect, and in the wake of this Rupert D'Oyly Carte immediately closed the Company down. Suddenly every performer on the books, both longstanding and otherwise, was out of work.

18

Where did that leave Leonard? As with other young men in the Company he expected to be called up for the Armed Services sooner or later. But he had to find some sort of work to keep him occupied in the interim, and apart from singing and acting, what other sort of work was he qualified for? The most obvious answer was something scientific, and he soon obtained a scientific post, though not this time as a chemist but as a meteorologist at Shoeburyness in Essex.

The days, weeks and months that followed the outbreak of war, though, saw little in the way of actual fighting. Nor did those weeks and months see the bombing of civilian targets which is what the Government had particularly feared. It was the period that came to be called the Phoney War. After less than a fortnight the theatres were allowed to re-open. The D'Oyly Carte Company eventually reassembled. And on Christmas Day of all surprising days, they began their wartime performing with a four week season in Edinburgh.

Leonard, however, was not among the performers who reassembled straight away, but his return to the Company was not to be delayed for long. On December 28th he wrote to Richard Collet, the D'Oyly Carte General Manager, to say he would be handing in his notice to his new employers three days later and would be "free to rejoin the Company any time after January 31st". And he was duly back with them when they opened a three week season at Golders Green Hippodrome in North London on February 5th.

Now until the end of this first wartime tour in July he regularly played the Defendant and, as another step up, he had been asked to give a "trial performance" (or maybe even two) of Earl Tolloller in *Iolanthe* during the season at Golders Green. "Trial performances", generally unpaid, were used by the Cartes as a way of checking whether a particular chorister/small part player was potential "principal" material. Leonard's chance had come, and he took it with both hands.

Had circumstances permitted, other trial performances might well have followed. At the end of May he asked to be considered for, and was given, a contract for the next tour beginning on August 12th. But in July his expected call-up papers at last arrived. He was ordered to report to Blackpool on August 7th for "service in the RAF". So off he went, sent on his way by a heartening letter from Richard Collet.

"Mr D'Oyly Carte" (*wrote Collet*) "was very pleased with the performance you gave of Tolloller. And if, at the end of hostilities, you want to take up this work again, I do not think there is any question that there is a future for you in this particular kind of work."

But Collet knew – Leonard knew – everybody knew – the new Prime Minister, Winston Churchill, had effectively told them so – hostilities were not going to end for a long time yet.

Of Leonard's wartime career we have, unfortunately, no more than glimpses. Presumably he passed his initial medical examination easily enough. Even so he can't in medical terms have been A1, for after a second examination in

December 1941 he was recorded as having a perforated ear drum and was marked down for "permanent home service" and "ground duties". Not for him would there be any sorties or bombing raids over Germany.

Nevertheless he was commissioned in the RAF Regiment as "Flight-Lieutenant 123647, Osborn, L.A.G." the following June. The RAF Regiment had been formed that February for airfield defence, and Leonard would have commanded an airfield unit. For a considerable period he was stationed for this purpose in Northern Ireland; and one evening while there he was caught on the end of the runway just as a fully laden squadron of Lancaster bombers was taking off. The noise of this would have been tremendous, and the result was to leave him completely deaf for several weeks.

Where else was he stationed during these years? One answer was the Isle of Man. Another was in, or somewhere near, Canterbury. While according to a brief summary of his life that in later years would appear in certain D'Oyly Carte programmes, he spent part of the war in Iceland. This was not impossible - British forces were sent to that country in May 1940. But given that he'd been designated for home postings only, it seems more likely that "Iceland" was simply a misprint for "Ireland".

But wherever he was at any given time, his days weren't totally spent on service activities. He still managed to find opportunities to sing. During his time in Canterbury, for instance, he sang at weekends in the Cathedral choir and also gave "recitals in the Cathedral". On November 8th 1944 – to take just one example – he and a pianist presented a programme that included a recitative and aria from Handel's oratorio *Esther*, and "The Smith" and the famous "Lullaby" by Brahms.

And something else in his life – something unconnected with either the war itself or with singing – happened during these years too. On June 27th 1942, the day after he'd been commissioned, he got married. His bride was Eileen Victoria Newman, a girl he had met from time to time at family parties. She originally worked for Peter Jones, the Oxford Street department store, as a seamstress doing dress alterations. During the war she had become a telephone operator with the GPO, and was recorded on their marriage certificate as being a "civil servant". She was then just two days short of her twenty-sixth birthday. Leonard himself was then twenty-seven, and was simply recorded as being in the RAF. The wedding took place in Tooting Parish Church.

A wartime wedding meant, of course, the possibility of instant separation for the couple concerned. But at least for Leonard and Eileen the periods of separation were not as lengthy as were those of so many of their contemporaries. They established their first home in Wallington near Croydon in Surrey, and Leonard must have got back there from time to time, as over the next three years two sons were born to them: Anthony Philip (Tony) on April 20th 1943 and Martin Robert on September 10th 1945.

And by the time Martin came along the war was over, and a start was slowly being made by the Government and everyone else to get things back to peacetime normality.

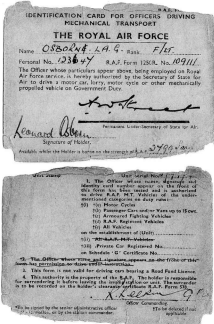

Flight-Lieutenant Osborn L.A.G.
(Melvyn Tarran and David Mackie collections)

Principal Tenor, 1946-48

Sometime early in 1946 Leonard was demobbed. And now, unlike the time when he'd first entered the jobs market, or that time in 1939 when the D'Oyly Carte Company had abruptly closed down, there was no interim period to be spent as a chemist, a meteorologist or in any other scientific capacity. Instead he made an immediate return to D'Oyly Carte. He was now thirty-one, and Rupert D'Oyly Carte, having given him another audition to re-check his voice and capabilities after so long, was clearly ready to have him back.

So after another spell with Maud Evans to remind him what D'Oyly Carte was all about and get him singing G&S again, and a number of sessions with Anna Bethell who the following year became the Company's new Stage Director, he rejoined the ranks. Initially he did so as a chorister once again, and for spells of just two or three days at a time, though with a salary doubled from four pounds a week to eight pounds and, even more enticing, the prospect of speedy promotion if things went well.

Accordingly he was asked to do a few more trial shows: as Marco in *The Gondoliers*; as Colonel Fairfax in *The Yeomen of the Guard*; as Nanki-Poo in *The Mikado* (twice; the only occasions, as it turned out, that he was to play Nanki-Poo in his entire D'Oyly Carte career); and another two as Earl Tolloller in *Iolanthe*. These trial shows duly had the desired outcome. Before long he had been appointed one of the principal tenors for the Company's next annual tour beginning early in September.

The Company to which he'd returned was both much the same as, yet in some respects very different from, that which he'd left six years before. It was very much a time of transition, with new blood gradually coming in to replace several of the older performers who had loyally stuck it out during the war years but who were now ready, or getting ready, to retire.

Though not *all* the older performers. John Dean was about to go (John Dudley had left in the summer of 1939); but among the team of principals of which Leonard had now become a member there remained three of almost venerable standing. Darrell Fancourt was still making his presence felt as strongly as ever. So was Leslie Rands. So was Richard Walker who, like the other two, went back to the 1920s and who, since 1943, had been principal heavy baritone in place of Sydney Granville. And there were a further two who, though junior by comparison, still went back to the last years of the 1930s: Helen Roberts, one of the two principal sopranos, and Ella Halman, the principal contralto.

These five were an imposing bunch in themselves, and now for the new (1946-47) tour another, still more imposing figure whose D'Oyly Carte origins went back to the '20s returned to the Company: Martyn Green who, like Leonard, had spent most of the war years in the RAF. Right from the start of his time as a principal, therefore, Leonard knew just how much he had to do in every part he played if he was to reach the standing and gain the popularity achieved by each and all of *them*.

So – what parts was he given?

The operas the Company took on this new tour were *The Mikado, The Gondoliers, The Yeomen of the Guard, Iolanthe, The Pirates of Penzance, Patience, Trial by Jury* plus, at the end of the tour, *HMS Pinafore*, the last of these played for the first time since 1940. And each of them has, of course, a leading tenor role.

These roles, though, are a long way from all being identical. Even allowing for the basic style in which, in D'Oyly Carte terms, they were always played, their range and compass vary considerably. Some of them – Ralph Rackstraw in *Pinafore* and Frederic in *Pirates*, for instance, or *Iolanthe's* Tolloller and the Duke of Dunstable in *Patience*, or Richard Dauntless in *Ruddigore* and Cyril in *Princess Ida* – have certain similarities both dramatically and musically. But in every case the differences between any two of them are at least as important as the similarities, and those differences were often strongly reflected in the performances of the various tenors who played them for the Company down the years.

Throughout its history – or at any rate since it had become purely a touring Company in 1909 – the management always made sure it had two principal tenors in its ranks, dividing the relevant parts between them sometimes equally, sometimes not. Despite this, the belief has occasionally been expressed that the parts have always been divided in the same way, with one of the tenors taking what, roughly speaking, may be called the romantic parts (Alexis in *The Sorcerer*, Ralph Rackstraw, Frederic, Hilarion in *Princess Ida*, Nanki-Poo, Fairfax and Marco) and the other the laddish and character parts (the Duke of Dunstable, Tolloller, Cyril and Dick Dauntless, along with the Defendant in *Trial by Jury* and Box in *Cox and Box*). And this is strange because the D'Oyly Carte casting rarely divided them exclusively on lines like that, but took in a variety of other factors as well.

So for this tour Leonard was given the parts of Fairfax and Marco from the first category, and the Duke of Dunstable and the Defendant from the second; while the other principal tenor took on Frederic, Nanki-Poo, Luiz in *The Gondoliers* and eventually Ralph Rackstraw from the first category but also Tolloller from the second. That other principal tenor's name was Thomas Round.

Leonard Osborn and Thomas Round. It's possible to argue that the two of them were the best tenor duo D'Oyly Carte ever had or, if not the very best, then surely *one* of the best. As a pairing they had a unique glamour, both being periodically described, in the honeyed phrase of the time, as "matinee idols" and both acquiring an ever-growing number of fans.

My impression – though I must stress it's only an impression - is that the fans formed two separate groups; that the most ardent fans of one were not necessarily the most ardent fans of the other. And if this was the case it wasn't totally surprising, for both on stage and off it they were very different. Let's consider Thomas Round (or "Tom" Round, as he was and still is widely known) first.

Thomas Round was Leonard's junior by just a year. An ex-policeman, he had spent much of the war as a flying instructor in America, and in 1946 was a newcomer not only to D'Oyly Carte but effectively to the professional stage as a whole. Despite this, however, he was made a principal within a few months of joining the Company, and there's no doubt that he was an instant success.

He was, before anything else, a singer. While he would always cope adequately with the demands of G&S and other musical theatre taken as a whole, it was essentially his voice which had got him where he was then, and would take him to an ever increasing number of heights and triumphs in the years ahead. His voice was not a big one, but it was one that he knew, or quickly learned, to use to the best advantage, a voice that was always pleasant and easy to listen to, a reliable voice and a voice that was technically first-rate.

His vocal prowess was immediately recognised by Helen Roberts, whose voice was also technically first-rate, who sang Mabel to his Frederic and Josephine to his Ralph, and who was particularly gratified when he came on the scene. Not only did their voices blend well but, she has said, "it was so nice to play opposite a *tall* tenor".

His height – five foot eleven and a half – plus a ready smile, an obvious friendliness, a sense he gave of being at ease with himself, and a trim, personable appearance were other factors that helped him along. "Good voice. Sings well. Nice type of man" was the way it was put on his Company audition card. And in terms of parts he was always at his best as the archetypal romantic tenor, the by-definition attractive figure who may fail to get the girl in Act One, but who you know is pretty well guaranteed to have done so by the time of the final curtain. In roles of this sort where a lightness of touch is crucial and acting of no great subtlety is required, he could more or less be himself. And he duly *was* more or less himself in the four romantic parts which he played during his first few years in D'Oyly Carte.

Now Leonard. By contrast with his fellow tenor, Leonard was as much an actor as he was a singer, probably more so; and had his career taken a different turn, he might have made a name for himself as an actor without doing any singing at all. At least one of his later D'Oyly Carte colleagues thought he would have done well in Shakespeare.

Like Thomas Round he was tall – six foot, according to his audition record – and with looks and a personality that have been enthusiastically described as, among other things, "handsome", "virile", "robust", "vigorous", "dashing", "manly" and "full-blooded". "He would light up immediately he got on stage," as one admirer has put it. "He had an exuberance and a sort of rugged

Leonard as Marco
(Melvyn Tarran collection)

masculinity that was far opposed to the typical sweetness of D'Oyly Carte's leading tenors," as another fan has written, the sort of masculinity (and looks) that add up unmistakably to sex appeal, and are envied by most of us who know we haven't got that sort of appeal ourselves. Envied, but in his case envied without jealousy or resentment, for it's one of the most striking things about him that his fans included any number of men as well as the legions of female fans he more obviously attracted; and the prime reason for this can be summed up in one word I've used in his connection already: charisma.

Charisma: how do you define it? The *Oxford English Dictionary* defines it as "a gift or power of leadership or authority; hence the capacity to inspire devotion or enthusiasm" – though that seems almost to underplay it. It's a facet of personality, a special "something" that, in theatrical terms, makes you unable to take your eyes off those performers who have it whenever they're on stage, even if they're in a crowd and even when they're doing nothing in particular. We can all think of performers who have singularly lacked charisma. Leonard had it in spades.

It came through in every part he played. "I once" (this is Chris Webster) "asked a devoted follower of the D'Oyly Carte from the 1920s onwards what she thought about Osborn. Her eyes misted over as she said 'Dear Leonard, he was marvellous'. To her and to a couple of other elderly ladies who joined the conversation, 'Dear Leonard' was a more charismatic performer than Derek Oldham." And that, coming from anyone of the interwar vintage, was really saying something.

Of the four parts he played on the 1946-47 tour, Marco was the one he found the most demanding and difficult. This was firstly because the character is on stage for well over half the opera, but even more crucially because he sails through everything that happens to him with bubbling insouciance and no real drama. The actor in Leonard preferred his stage characters to have more to them than that, and for this reason he particularly relished playing Colonel Fairfax whose character is much more fully drawn. "Fairfax," he said, "is wonderful from the acting point of view" – though he relished almost as much what he called the "lovely little cameo part" of the Duke of Dunstable.

But it was principally his performances as Marco and Fairfax that initially attracted the most attention from the newspaper critics, and his name featured pretty well as a matter of course in their reviews of the two operas in which these characters appear. Here are just three examples from that first tour:

"Leonard Osborn is a romantic Fairfax, with a sense of humour too."
(*Yorkshire Evening Press*, York)

"The two gondoliers, whose identity causes so much bother, fell to Leonard Osborn and Leslie Rands. Probably 'Take a Pair of Sparkling Eyes' [Marco's song] was the most applauded song during the evening."
(*Eastern Daily Press*, Norwich)

Leonard as Colonel Fairfax – first costume

"Leonard Osborn makes a gallant Fairfax, and perhaps [scores] the biggest success vocally of the present production."

(Eastern Daily Press again)

And from the same paper two years later:

"The gay and gallant Fairfax of Leonard Osborn last night had in it something of the panache of the young soldiers with handlebar moustaches and corduroy trousers who fought in the Western Desert."

The sense of humour mentioned in the first of these notices is worth stressing. And even more important to stress are the two references to his singing voice. If his singing voice was to become, so to speak, his eventual Achilles' heel, there is no suggestion in any of the above of vocal deficiencies. Rather it's clear that on this first tour he was vocally on top form. Since his return to civilian life he had resumed singing lessons, though with a different teacher from the one he'd had before, and this may well have contributed to the finished effect.

That said, however, it must also be said – and there's probably no arguing about this – that his voice was less technically assured than that of Thomas Round. It almost certainly failed to impress Helen Roberts who, as Elsie Maynard and Gianetta, played opposite him in *The Yeomen of the Guard* and *The Gondoliers*. It also lacked Round's smoothness of delivery. But it was a very distinctive voice, a voice he projected well, a voice agreeable in tone, a voice that matched his vibrant personality; and, most important of all, a voice that could lift a whole performance.

For myself, I remember above all in this respect his singing of the first verse of the trio "Of all the young Ladies I know" shortly after his first entrance when he came regularly to play Tolloller. In particular, the exhilarating strength and power that he put into the repeat of the line "Her origin's lowly, it's true" made this trio, while he was in the Company, my favourite number in *Iolanthe*. The effect he achieved may not have come over fully in his eventual recording of the number, but that's another matter. There's no doubt in my mind about its effect in the theatre.

Presumably because, unlike Thomas Round, he had been in the Company before the war, he now regarded himself as the *senior* tenor, but it's by no means certain that Rupert D'Oyly Carte also regarded him that way. This was reflected, first, by the respective salaries he initially paid them – fifteen pounds rising to twenty pounds a week in the case of Round, against fifteen pounds full stop in the case of Leonard. But just as significant were the parts he'd asked each of them to play when looked at in terms of the operas in which those parts featured, and the relative number of performances each opera was given.

Taking the years 1946-59 as a whole (the years, that is, that encompassed Leonard's time as a principal) there was no question which of the operas were performed most often. Top of the list, as in all the years before Leonard's time and after his time too, was, of course, *The Mikado*. Second – at least until the

Leonard as Colonel Fairfax – second costume

second half of the 1970s – was *The Gondoliers*. Third and fourth, roughly equal, came *The Yeomen of the Guard* and *Iolanthe*, and fifth *The Pirates of Penzance* – with *HMS Pinafore*, *Patience* and, when it returned to the repertoire, *Ruddigore* lagging some way behind.

And the fact that for their first tour Thomas Round was given parts in both *The Mikado* and *The Gondoliers* (even accepting that Luiz in the latter opera is a more or less secondary part), *plus* a part in *Iolanthe*, *plus* a part in *The Pirates of Penzance* meant that he (Round) had considerably more performances in which to shine than Leonard, who had parts in only two of the top five operas.

The 1946-47 tour divided itself into three phases. The first phase, lasting from September to mid-January, was a typical D'Oyly Carte autumn and early winter tour. The third part, from April onwards, was an equally typical spring and summer one. But the middle phase – the depths of winter phase stretching roughly from mid-January to the end of March - was anything but typical. For this was the winter of the great British freeze-up, when the whole country was covered deep in snow, and the Arctic conditions were made still worse by an acute shortage of coal.

Everyone suffered. And the members of the D'Oyly Carte Company suffered as much as anyone else, having to perform in bitterly cold theatres, go back after the performances to bitterly cold digs, and travel from town to town in bitterly cold trains. Everyone in the Company had his or her particular memories of those freezing times. For example – Martyn Green, in his autobiography:

> "I well remember a performance of *Patience* when, as Bunthorne, and wearing my velvet suit, I found it difficult not to shiver myself off the stump on which I was sitting."

Thomas Round, in *his* autobiography:

> "The Company moved on [from Hull] to Sunderland … and it never stopped snowing. Electricity was being cut off, and we had to make up by candlelight at the Empire Theatre."

Ella Halman, in some unpublished recollections, referring to the week they played Huddersfield, where

> "the dressing rooms were under the stage and appeared to be carved out of stone. I only remember one small one-bar electric fire down there, and all the girls were frozen when we played *Iolanthe* in those scanty clothes. The only bearable place was actually on the stage, under the lights."

And this to his readers from a columnist in the *Eastern Evening News* when they played Norwich:

"Despite the many difficulties [from which the Company] are suffering, I heard only one complaint. That was from one of the principals who had lost her hot water bottle – a very important part of equipment for a travelling actress these days.

If anyone has such a means of comfort to spare, he can earn the gratitude of a delightful soprano who has spent a large proportion of her spare time since arriving in Norwich in hunting for one.

I ought to add that the lady rules out the stone and metal varieties."

Hot water bottles made of stone or metal? Well, this *was* 1947.

Leonard's own experiences that winter and his feelings about it are not recorded. But one thing may be said with certainty: that he would have chafed at the fact that during all those weeks the snow had prevented him playing golf.

So what was the significance of golf?

When I asked Tony Osborn whether his father had had any off duty pastimes, his response was simply "golf". When in the mid-1950s Leonard filled in that form giving details about himself for the use of the D'Oyly Carte office (see page 12), a form that included space for listing "interests and hobbies", he likewise simply put "golf". He was one of at least a dozen golfers among the male members of the Company at this time, the others including Martyn Green, a true golfing fanatic, Darrell Fancourt, Thomas Round, and the chief tenor understudy, Thomas Hancock, another figure who was back in the Company after war service.

Golf, as Thomas Round was quickly informed when *he* joined the Company, was "a good form of exercise for singers" as well as being a good thing to play from a socialising point of view. Indeed "The D'Oyly Carte Golf Circle", as it was more or less officially called, dated back to the 1920s if not before. At any number of towns in which the Company performed, the golfers were accorded honorary temporary membership of the local golf club; and in return for the welcome and hospitality they received, they would give the club members a concert on a Sunday evening.

The 1946-47 tour ended with a four week season at Sadler's Wells concluding on August 16th. And for Leonard that tour, his first tour as a D'Oyly Carte principal, had undoubtedly been a success. If newspaper reviews were one proof of this, if audience reaction to his performances was another, a third – the strongest proof of all – came when, for the next (1947-48) tour, Rupert D'Oyly Carte upped his salary from fifteen pounds a week to twenty pounds.

But while, on the one hand, he recognised that things were going well, he also made clear early in the new tour that he wasn't entirely happy with the way they were shaping with regard to the days and weeks ahead. The highlight of the new tour was to be a five month visit to America beginning in December; and on October 24th he wrote a letter to Rupert D'Oyly Carte about the distribution of the tenor parts that was to operate on that visit.

"Dear Mr Carte (*he began*)
I thank you for your letter of the 17th October notifying me that you

are exercising the option on my services as per Clause 15 of my Agreement.

I should like at this time to remind you of the very brief conversation we had at Sadler's Wells at the end of the last tour concerning the possibility of my playing a performance of Ralph in *Pinafore* before the Company goes to America. As I pointed out then, if I do have to play it in America, as a member of the cast I shall be judged as a principal and not as an understudy, and I'd much prefer to prepare for it and do it now, than go on at a moment's notice in America.

There was also mentioned the question of more work for me to do. It is true that *Cox and Box* is keeping me busy at present in the rehearsal stage [prior to its return to the repertoire for the first time since the war] but as things are I have more shows off than on. By the end of Edinburgh [November 8th] I shall have played this tour twenty-four performances to Mr Round's thirty-two. Besides this I shall have played twelve performances of Defendant to Mr Round's eleven performances of Luiz – small parts which are pretty even.

As I suggested at the time, were I to play Tolloller, this would even up the number of performances that we each play. As you know, I played two performances of Tolloller at Hammersmith in 1946 and I also gave a trial show of it for you in 1940 before I joined the RAF.

> Yours sincerely
> Leonard Osborn."

This is the earliest letter of Leonard's that I've quoted in full, and in many ways it's a letter that was very characteristic. It was fluently written and well expressed. It argued its case clearly and kept to the point. It was businesslike in tone without being rigidly so. But at the same time it showed two things about him that were distinctly at variance with the debonair personality and smiling face he presented to his audiences and fans; and, as will become apparent from other letters to be quoted in the chapters ahead, these things were as much a side of him as his debonair and smiling side.

First of them was his concern with his status as a principal. Here was the boy from a humble background, a boy who had not had status conferred upon him by birth or upbringing, but who had had to work for it, to earn it as he'd earned it at school; and who, having achieved it, felt driven thereafter to make sure he held on to it.

And second, very much related to this, was a readiness to jump in and question decisions made about him by people in authority if he felt he was being hard done by at any time.

Both these things – concern with status and a willingness to assert himself with those in authority – suggest that he suffered from an underlying sense of insecurity. Was he a person who suffered from a sense of insecurity? This was another of the questions I asked his son. "Yes," said Tony Osborn, "I think he was." Barry Pendry, in his report on his character as revealed by his handwriting, puts the point another way. Leonard, he suggests, was a person "intent on proper organisation, self-protecting by insisting upon the game being played according to the rules."

Did the letter have any effect? The answer, perhaps surprisingly given what was essentially the autocratic D'Oyly Carte approach to management – that performers were simply employees who were expected to know their place – was yes; or at least yes to some extent. Rupert Carte pencilled a note on it: "Speak to Miss Bethell about this" – that is, Anna Bethell as Stage Director. Leonard got nowhere with his request to play Ralph Rackstraw. Ralph was to be the one principal tenor part in the immediate post-war repertoire that he was never to play on stage in all his years in the Company.

But he got his wish as regards Tolloller. Tolloller was one of the six parts he was to play in America.

The American visit of 1947-48 marked a further step on the Company's road back to the way things had been pre-war. Yet at the same time it was a step that presented a considerable challenge. The three American visits of the 1930s had been glamorous, high profile affairs which had proved outstandingly successful in every respect. But nine years had passed since the last visit – the visit on which Leonard had gone as a chorister – and the world had changed a lot since then. Would the Company achieve the same success now?

They were certainly given a prestigious send-off – nothing less than an official farewell party at the Savoy Hotel. Then they headed by train for Southampton where they were to embark for their transatlantic voyage on the no less prestigious and superbly appointed *Queen Mary*. If they could have had a smooth crossing, it would really have set the seal on things, but a totally smooth crossing was not within even the *Queen Mary's* power to provide.

They arrived, moreover, to find themselves in the thick of the American winter. It was Christmas Eve; and having endured the snow and blizzards of an icy winter the year before at home, they now encountered the same conditions in New York. But there was one great difference – or perhaps two. Whereas at home, thanks to the desperate shortage of fuel, they had felt frozen both indoors and out, they found in New York every building centrally heated.

And added to that were the pleasures and delights of being in a city where the shops were brightly lit and laden with goods – laden in a way that shops back in Britain had not been laden for years. Leonard took particular advantage of this by sending Christmas hampers home – hampers "containing all sorts of wonders". But one of the wonders in one of the hampers didn't reach the people it was intended for. When his sister Mabel received a hamper for herself and her family, she "removed the chewing gum" before her son Kenneth or any other youthful hands could get it in their grasp.

But it was not for the shops that the Company were primarily in New York. They were there to present G&S, and they gave their opening performance on December 29th. They had brought with them their full repertoire: seven two act operas, plus their two curtain-raisers, and that December evening they started off with *The Mikado*. It wasn't, however, the best evening in D'Oyly Carte history. They were playing the New Century Theatre, a somewhat less welcoming house than the Martin Beck Theatre which they had played in the

D'OYLY CARTE OPERA COMPANY

To-night's Programme will be taken from the following Selections :—

1. ORCHESTRAL SELECTIONS
   Geraldo's Orchestra (*Conductor:* SYDNEY KENNEDY)

2. FULL COMPANY...."The Merriest Fellows,"
   ACT I, "GONDOLIERS"

3. MISS MURIEL HARDING...."Maids of Cadiz"....DELIBES

4. MR. DONALD HARRIS.."The Watchman"..W. H. SQUIRES

5. MISS JOAN GILLINGHAM......"Ava Maria"......GOUNOD

6. MR. C. WILLIAM MORGAN
   MR. LEONARD OSBORN   *Trio:* "If You Go In"
   MR. PETER PRATT   ACT II, "IOLANTHE"

7. MISS CARYL FANE.."Oh Foolish Fay"..ACT II, "IOLANTHE"

8. MR. THOMAS ROUND
   Serenade from "Fair Maid of Perth"....BIZET

9. MISS GWYNETH CULLIMORE
   MISS DENISE FINDLAY   *Quartette:*
   MR. CHARLES DORNING   "Regular Royal Queen"
   MR. LEONARD OSBORN   ACT I, "GONDOLIERS"

---

10. *INTERVAL*   *COLLECTION*
    Selection — ORCHESTRA

---

11. FULL COMPANY........"Hail Poetry"
    ACT I, "PIRATES OF PENZANCE"

12. MR. PETER PRATT .... *Song*

13. MISS DENISE FINDLAY ...... "I Love Thee" ...... GRIEG

14. MR. RICHARD DUNN and MR. LEONARD OSBORN
    Duet: "Cox and Box"

15. MR. CHARLES DORNING...."Prologue from Pagliacci"
    LEON CAVALLO

16. MISS HELEN ROBERTS .... *Song*

17. MR. ERIC HUTSON .... "Water Boy" .... AVERY ROBINSON

18. MR. LEONARD OSBORN.."Take a Pair of Sparkling Eyes"
    SULLIVAN

19. *FINALE*—FULL COMPANY .... ACT II, "GONDOLIERS"

NATIONAL ANTHEMS

A D'Oyly Carte concert on board the *Queen Mary*

34

'30s, and the performance itself fell somewhat flat. It was "an undistinguished *Mikado*," wrote the critic from the *New York Times*.

But after a week of *The Mikado* came a week of *Trial* and *Pirates*, and with *Trial* and *Pirates* the Company got into their stride and all feelings of flatness were forgotten. Now the *New York Times* was describing them as being "in fine fettle" and the double bill as being brilliantly sung, and the success of the visit was assured.

Leonard, of course, had not appeared in *The Mikado* and, as in 1939, he made his initial bow of the visit as the Defendant in *Trial by Jury*. Thereafter he eventually played each of his other parts; and if his name didn't crop up as much or as fulsomely as it might have done in the reviews, it nonetheless came to the attention of certain influential people in the wider world of stage musicals. After seventeen weeks in New York the Company moved on to Boston. And from Boston on May 4th (1948) he wrote another letter to Rupert D'Oyly Carte. As in his earlier letter about Ralph Rackstraw and Tolloller, he brought up the question of his status in the Company and, this time, a concern about his salary as well. But this time he also wrote in what reads like a state of considerable excitement and in terms that suggested he believed he held a fairly strong card:

"Dear Mr Carte
    I don't know whether it has reached the ears of the London office yet, but whether it has or not, I feel that you would prefer to hear it from me.
    I have been offered a part in a new Cole Porter/Bella Spewack musical comedy here in America. I state quite emphatically that so far it is still only an offer; I have seen no contract, or anything in writing, yet.
    However the agent – Richard LaMarr of A&S Lyons, Inc. – has suggested to me that a contract of four hundred dollars per week would be within the bounds of possibility. Taking into consideration the standing and popularity of Cole Porter, and also of Bella Spewack, I feel that it would be a 'safe' bet to accept.
    I also feel inclined to accept after considering your offer of a further engagement at the same terms of twenty pounds per week. Before this American offer came along I was determined to ask you for more work, to be the principal tenor at an increased salary; but I also knew that Mr Round felt the same way, and that there was no room for both of us on 'equal' terms. I cannot afford to be the minor of the two tenors, and I am unwilling to take that chance.
    I would prefer – infinitely prefer – to be the principal tenor in the D'Oyly Carte Opera Company to being the juvenile lead in a Cole Porter show in America, even with all its possibilities.
    This American production does not go into rehearsal until the middle of September, and so I shall be available for the [June-July] Sadler's Wells season. In the meantime, however, I should like to hear from you if possible. Even though you have nothing better to offer me

than as you stated in your letter, at least that I may receive your blessing."

"*I cannot afford to be the minor of the two tenors.*" As a statement of his position he could hardly have put things more succinctly. Was it, then, to be the end of his time in D'Oyly Carte?

It might have been. But - happily - it wasn't, partly because for whatever reason or combination of reasons, the American offer came to nothing. Yet it did perhaps alert Rupert Carte to the gap that would be created in the Company if Leonard were now to leave. At all events, he upped his salary for the second year in succession, raising it by no less than fifty per cent from twenty pounds a week to thirty pounds, the same salary he would now be paying Thomas Round.

It is interesting, though, to speculate what his place in D'Oyly Carte history would have been had he actually left the Company at this point, and the answer is not hard to guess. He would have gone down as just one of the many performers over the years (tenors and sopranos especially) who came, did reasonably well or even *very* well while they were there, but who then departed and became little more than vague names from the past. "Leonard Osborn? Oh yes, I remember. Fairfax – Marco – the Duke in *Patience*. Yes, he was first-class. But I'm not sure I remember anything more about him than that."

All this, though, was about to change. Over the next twelve months or so something happened that ensured he would gain a place in the D'Oyly Carte gallery of performers that was all his own. That "something" was the chance to play what in a sense was a completely new part. The part in question was Dick Dauntless. And the chance to play it came about because that year, 1948, for the first time since the war, the Company were reviving *Ruddigore*.

Leonard as the Duke of Dunstable

36

"Ease, Security and Confidence", 1948-51

Ruddigore, as every Gilbert and Sullivan aficionado knows, had a chequered career. Right from its first night in January 1887 it somehow became set apart from the rest of the G&S canon. When its initial London run closed after less than ten months, it was even dismissed in some quarters as a failure, and the word "failure" was hung round its neck as if it were the operatic equivalent of an infectious disease.

For more than three decades after that opening run it was the one opera in the main G&S sequence that was never revived either in London or by any of the Carte companies touring the provinces. But when in 1920 Rupert D'Oyly Carte at last brought it back, its fortunes took an upturn of astonishing proportions. For a time it became enormously popular, to the extent that during the 1920s as a whole it was played more than any of the other operas except the top four. Now it was to be brought back again, and with new costumes and sets. The designer of the new costumes and the set for Act Two was a man named Peter Goffin.

Peter Goffin had first become associated with the Company shortly before the war when Rupert Carte had commissioned him to re-design the costumes and set for *The Yeomen of the Guard*. His costumes for *Yeomen* had been received with reasonable favour. But when it came to his set, "favour" was emphatically not the word, or not with most of the D'Oyly Carte regulars. His efforts had been described as everything from drab and characterless to clumsy and the theatrical equivalent of vandalism. And whether any given person liked them or not, they were certainly controversial.

With *Ruddigore*, though, Goffin avoided any major controversy, and the designs he came up with in this instance were mostly received with approval. One of their strongest suits was colour, especially in the costumes. "Even in days of plenty," a critic in Manchester was to write on first seeing those costumes, they would have stood out. In the late 1940s – those years of grim austerity – they blazed with "colours the eye looks on hungrily: bold reds, mossy greens, delicate azures we had forgotten".

Leonard, as Dick Dauntless, largely missed out on this new *Ruddigore* colour. His costume as "a man-o'-war's-man" did undergo a certain change. Previously Dauntless's jacket had been bright blue and his trousers white. Now both were dark. But that was the only thing on which he did miss out, unless you count the fact that Dauntless has relatively little to do in the second act. Otherwise the revival of the opera and his part in it worked triumphantly in his favour.

For a start, there was the fact that the part was given to *him* – to him, that is, rather than to Thomas Round. Then there were the possibilities inherent in the part itself. Those possibilities had been duly seized on by most of the performers who had played it previously: Durward Lely who created it, for example, and Derek Oldham, Leo Darnton and Charles Goulding who had been three of its leading exponents in the interwar years. Each in his way had made a considerable success of it. Yet the success Leonard himself was to make of it was a success of a higher and more sublime order than even the four of *them* had managed.

It helped, of course, that it was a part that fitted him to perfection. All the "masculine" adjectives used to describe his performances in general (see page 24) could be used to describe his laddish seaman with still more justification. In the opinion of no less a figure than Darrell Fancourt, who had seen all the interwar exponents of the part, Leonard was "the greatest Dauntless ever". It was – and remained – his favourite part.

But there was more to it even than that. His success in the part was a success that in D'Oyly Carte history was unique, and its uniqueness can be expressed like this. Take any other D'Oyly Carte performer of any period. And having done so, if you were then to ask (say) half a dozen people who had seen that performer on stage "what was his or her best part?" the chances are you would get three or four different answers at least. But if you asked the same question about Leonard you could guarantee that – what? – nineteen people out of twenty would give you the same answer: Dick Dauntless.

I can't think of anyone else who came near him in this respect. Charles Goulding had gone some way towards it with *his* Dick Dauntless, but it wasn't any more than that; people were as likely to say his best part was Fairfax or Marco. The only possible contender, it seems to me, was Darrell Fancourt with his portrayal of the Mikado, a portrayal once described as "monstrously imaginative" and "one of the great creations of our time". But even this wasn't quite the same. The Mikado was universally agreed to have been Fancourt's defining part. But it doesn't follow that virtually everyone who saw him play it regarded it as his *best* part.

It can also be said that, in the memory of most people who saw Leonard play Dauntless, two facets of his performance stood out in particular; and the first of these was his first entrance "from the briny sea" about twenty-five minutes into the opera. Here's how it's described by Geoffrey Dixon:

"He had a first act entrance that knocked 'em in the aisles. He used to vault the railings at the back of the set"

Leonard as Dick Dauntless, dancing the hornpipe
(Photograph: Houston Rogers)

by Michael Butler:

"His first entrance in Act One was breathtaking as he leapt over the railing at the back of the stage"

by Jon Ellison:

"He made a dynamic first entrance, vaulting over the iron fence that was draped with fishing nets along the edge of the rear ramp"

and by Jeffrey Skitch:

"For his first entrance he used to do a quite spectacular leap down on to the stage."

But surpassing even that was the hornpipe he danced following his opening song – the song about the poor Parley-voo. The hornpipe, though it had been in the opera from the beginning, owed its inclusion not primarily to Gilbert or Sullivan themselves but to a chance remark made to Gilbert by Durward Lely. Gilbert had immediately taken the idea on board, Sullivan had then written an appropriate tune and, as Lely later wrote, the hornpipe was "the success of the opening night".

It's probably anyone's guess whether Leonard's ability as a dancer was a factor in Rupert D'Oyly Carte's and, presumably, Anna Bethell's decision to cast him in the part. The only dances in the parts he was already playing in the other operas were the cachucha and the gavotte in *The Gondoliers* and in the trio "If you go in" in *Iolanthe*. But *The Gondoliers* cachucha is a communal dance. It's not a dance in which any of the participants are required to stand out; while in the gavotte and the *Iolanthe* trio all the interest had traditionally come to be focused on the performer playing, respectively, the Duke of Plaza-Toro and the Lord Chancellor, not the performer playing Marco and Tolloller. By contrast with these dances, the *Ruddigore* hornpipe is a solo performance. Except for a certain amount of incidental back-up from the chorus of bridesmaids on stage with him, Dick Dauntless is out there on his own.

It seems unlikely that Leonard had ever danced a hornpipe before. He went for a number of lessons to learn how to dance it now. Those lessons cost him a total of one pound sixteen shillings, and the Company duly reimbursed him for his outlay. "I hope," he wrote in a letter acknowledging the reimbursement, "the hornpipe will justify the expense."

One pound sixteen was cheap at the price. To say the expense was justified was an almost ludicrous understatement. Here are just three examples of the comments that down the years his performance of the dance inspired:

He "jigs and hornpipes so lithely that the quality of his voice is nearly underestimated."

(*Manchester Evening News*, March 1949)

40

"The hornpipe gave great pleasure. It was interesting to see that Leonard Osborn has lost none of his skill."

(Oxford Times, June 1956)

And my definite favourite:

"Leonard Osborn did a hornpipe through the hearts of the village maidens like a destroyer cleaving through the sea."

(Nottingham Evening Post, August 1956)

It has even been suggested that his hornpipe became something that was famed among naval personnel themselves.

Another little cameo that became part of his performance is particularly treasured by Michael Butler:

"I also well remember the signalling used for encores of [Robin Oakapple's song] 'My Boy, you may take it from me'. Once Robin had finished the song and danced off into the wings, then, if an encore was granted, Leonard Osborn would indicate with a sweep of his hat that Robin should return. Once the last encore had been sung he would throw his hat to the ground – an indication to Robin to return to his dressing room."

The revived *Ruddigore* had its first performance in Newcastle on November 1st 1948, and was given prominence in the D'Oyly Carte repertoire for the rest of that year's tour. In five provincial towns it was even chosen for the opening performance, partly no doubt because this pretty well guaranteed it a review or reviews in the relevant local press; and, as already mentioned, it was performed on the first three nights of the Sadler's Wells season towards the end of the tour in the summer.

And though there was the odd review in which, curiously, Leonard failed to get even a mention, this didn't alter the significance of what had happened so far as he himself was concerned: that with Dick Dauntless he had gained D'Oyly Carte immortality; that his name in G&S was now made.

Something else of significance, though, had happened in 1948. On September 12th – that is, while *Ruddigore* was still in rehearsal – Rupert D'Oyly Carte had died. At the time the Company were playing Glasgow, and they were duly present *en bloc* at a memorial service for him held in Glasgow Cathedral. Leonard was unlikely to have been greatly upset by his death; few of the performers were unlikely to have been upset by it. Rupert Carte was always an aloof, reserved and remote figure, as emotionally detached from his performers as they were from him. His successor as head of the Company was his daughter Bridget.

But at least he'd been a known quantity. By contrast, so far as the Company were concerned, Bridget D'Oyly Carte was totally *un*known. Her previous career had been in the fields of interior design and social work. How would she be in a role for which, in almost every respect, she was unprepared? How in particular would she treat the performers? Her father had treated them austerely and to an extent ungenerously but not, in general, unfairly. Taking things as a whole he had treated Leonard fairly. Would Bridget treat him fairly too?

If the first twelve months and more of her regime were anything to go by, it seemed unlikely he'd have much to complain about. There were three things that pointed to this conclusion. First, following the pattern established by her father, she increased his salary, this time from thirty pounds a week to thirty-five pounds, for the new tour beginning in August 1949.

And if that was confirmation of his stature in the Company, so, in a different way, was pointer number two. At some stage during 1949 he began, for what appears to have been the first time, to have problems with his voice.

Those problems, moreover, were not only physical-cum-medical, but had developed into a mental problem too. Despite his huge success as Dick Dauntless, what was happening to his voice had brought about a disturbing drop in his self-confidence. And if he managed, as it seems he did, to disguise this drop in self-confidence from his audiences, it was clear to certain people in the Company that he needed some sort of help.

Accordingly, at the instigation of Bridget herself, he was put in touch with a Kensington-based voice specialist, H. Arnold Smith. And Smith proved exactly the man to clear the problems up. On October 1st he wrote to Bridget regarding the successful outcome of his intervention as reported to him by Alfred Nightingale, the Company's current General Manager:

"Dear Miss D'Oyly Carte

I was very pleased indeed to hear from Mr Nightingale, by phone, that your tenor vocalist Leonard Osborn has now started the new season, and is singing with such success that, in Mr Nightingale's words, his performances are proving 'terrific' – furthermore that he has gained tremendously in confidence.

I am sure you know that this report gave me the very greatest pleasure. The difficult situation you called me in to investigate proved, according to my diagnosis, to be due to two main reasons. Firstly, incorrect and strained production of his voice, and secondly to a very unhealthy throat condition (septic tonsils).

However, with my voice placing and healthy methods giving him ease, security and confidence, and the throat specialist's successful operation [taking those tonsils out] he should now develop into the very fine artist I felt he could become when I first heard his performance at Croydon.

I have pleasure in enclosing my professional account for the diagnosis and his lessons."

The problems were over – at least for the time being.

That Leonard's self-confidence had indeed been restored is indicated by another two letters written that autumn and winter, letters in both these cases penned by himself. The first of the two, dated September 25th, was sent to Alfred Nightingale, and its tone was not far short of jaunty:

"Dear Mr Nightingale

The prospect of four weeks in Hull over the Christmas and New Year seasons is not a bright one, especially as a large majority of the Opera Company will have no chance of getting away from Hull to spend any time with their families.

However, I am endeavouring to bring a bright spot to the stay in Hull with a Company party on Christmas Day at one of the hotels. The management of one of the hotels – the Manchester – is friendly with several of the boys and girls, and did in fact throw a little party for them last New Year's Eve.

On previous years the principals have given little parties in their several dressing rooms, or distributed largesse in the form of Christmas spirit – thirty-two and sixpence a bottle – and, having been approached, they have agreed to pool those monies for the one big party, thus necessitating only a nominal sum from the members who attend.

I mentioned the proposed party to Mr [Hugh] Jones, who suggested that I write you to find out whether there will be time off or not. I was rather expecting Christmas Day to be sandwiched in between the matinees of Saturday Christmas Eve and Monday Boxing Day. However, if there is to be time off over the Christmas [period] I shall still go ahead with the party for the following Sunday, New Year's Day. So will you please let me know as early as possible what the programme is for Hull, so that I can make the necessary arrangements.

I would also like you to let Miss Bridgette [sic] Carte know of this, so that we have the blessing and best wishes from the head office."

The desired blessing must have been bestowed and the best wishes given, for Leonard's second letter, written from Hull to Bridget direct, contains an account of the party itself. It's also the third pointer to Bridget's favourable attitude towards him as she sought to consolidate her own position in the Company:

"Dear Miss Carte

Mr Jones has today handed me your donation for the party that the principals gave to the Company on Christmas Day, and on behalf of those members who so enjoyed the party, I should like to say how much we appreciated your generous gesture.

Hull is not the brightest of places to spend Christmas Day, but I think all the boys and girls who came – there were forty-two of us altogether – thoroughly enjoyed themselves. We started off with cocktails and carols, then Christmas dinner with all the trimmings. When we were replete we were entertained for about thirty minutes by a conjuror-illusionist, and then on to party games and competitions.

43

Once again, many many thanks, and may I take this opportunity of wishing you a happy and prosperous New Year, with continued good health."

"Party games, competitions and a conjuror-illusionist." The whole thing has an endearing feel of innocence to it. But this *was*, after all, the world of 1949.

The episode, though, showed Leonard in a new role, the role of an organiser and a role that, as someone who had considered becoming a schoolmaster, clearly fitted his temperament – though whether he was cast in that role by "the boys and girls" or whether he cast himself in it is another matter. Either way it suggests a feeling of warmth on his part towards his colleagues in the Company, the people with whom he worked.

At some point, too, he became the person who organised the Sunday evening golf club concerts – on which occasions he himself would usually sing, *sotto voce*, "Greensleeves" and, with suitable vigour, "The Blue Bonnets are over the Border".

But allowing for this feeling of warmth towards his colleagues as a whole, what of his feelings towards particular individuals? Did he have any special friends in the ranks? According to Frederick Sinden, a tenor chorister who was to join the Company in 1950 and who became one of his understudies, he was one of a group that centred round the star of the whole show, Martyn Green. Sinden himself admired Martyn Green enormously, not to say worshipped him; and Leonard, he claims, worshipped him too. In an interview many years later, referring to the D'Oyly Carte principal comedians with whom he had worked personally, he (Leonard) said: "For me Martyn Green was the greatest. [As a performer] he could convince you of everything." Yet this didn't automatically make them as close as all that, and it seems likely that what had led Green to take him up was their mutual enthusiasm for golf.

But even this wasn't proof of a really deep friendship. And when I put the question "Did Leonard have any special friends in the Company?" to his son, the name Tony Osborn came up with was Alan Styler.

Eleven years Leonard's junior and an ex-Grenadier Guardsman, Alan Styler had joined D'Oyly Carte as a chorister in 1947. Two years later he was made a principal, taking over the light baritone roles – Giuseppe, Strephon, Pish-Tush and so forth – from a performer called Charles Dorning, who had previously taken them over from Leslie Rands.

"For Mr Styler," wrote one reviewer of a performance in which the latter had gone on as an understudy, "there should be a happy future. He has a strong, resonant voice and abundant confidence. In due course he will give the Gilbertian words and phrases their full value."

The part for which he was standing in on that occasion was Giuseppe, teaming up in the process with Leonard's Marco, and over a period of about four years they were to reign jointly as the two gondoliers on any number of other occasions. At times, too, they teamed up as Cox and Box, and as a pair they were very suitably matched. Both were tall (Styler was five foot ten), both

44

Alan Styler as Strephon
(Photograph: G&S Photos)

were good looking and both were stage "naturals". Styler had a "flair for the amusingly inflated", suggested one critic who saw him as Strephon, and he had his female fans, just as Leonard did. One American lady, an eager admirer of them both on stage, admitted after she'd met them in person that, while she'd found Leonard not quite as handsome as she'd been expecting, she thought Alan Styler was gorgeous, though – the one point against him – she was shocked to find that he smoked.

Yet smoking or non-smoking (and, as already indicated – see page 3 – Leonard smoked too; but then, who didn't in those days?) I think it's fair to say that he never quite had Leonard's charisma or performed with Leonard's energy and full-blooded intensity. He was too much of a joker, too relaxed a personality to take that extra leap that separates the good from the very good; and he never really fulfilled his early promise.

Tony Osborn, though, did offer a second name when responding to my question about Leonard's special friends. But in the case of this second name he used the word "friend" in a way I hadn't been thinking about. Leonard, he wrote, had an affair with a member of the Company called Margaret. This was certainly news to me. But was it correct?

And who was Margaret? Tony said he didn't know her surname. But there was only one Margaret in the Company at this time, so it didn't take long to establish her identity. She was Margaret Mitchell, and yes, she and Leonard did have an affair, and one that was sufficiently known about for the two of them to be openly recognised as a couple. Amazingly I got confirmation of this from two other sources only days after Tony Osborn had mentioned it in the first place.

So: Margaret Mitchell – or "Maggie" Mitchell as she was known in the Company – what of *her*? Born at Dollar in Central Scotland in 1927, she was one of those people who are never slow to put themselves forward – and that was exactly what she'd done when first approaching D'Oyly Carte. Somehow she had wangled an audition with the Company at the age of just fifteen and a half; and though told she was too young to be taken on then, she had clearly made an impression. Eighteen months later she was invited to audition again, and this time she was accepted. By the end of 1945, still in her teens, she had become one of the Company's two principal sopranos.

Sopranos for the most part play opposite tenors, though curiously she and Leonard didn't play opposite each other till the advent of *Ruddigore*, when she was cast as Rose Maybud to his Dick Dauntless. "Margaret Mitchell, whose voice last year was notable more for quantity than quality, has in the interval gained immensely in control and artistry," the magazine *Musical Opinion* wrote of her following *Ruddigore's* first performances at Sadler's Wells. "Her Rose Maybud was well conceived, coy and attractive and vocally beyond reproach."

As for her appearance, she is described by Frederick Sinden as "a cracker – a gorgeous looking girl", and that when as Casilda in *The Gondoliers* it came to the moment when she receives a compliment from Don Alhambra, she "fluttered her eyelashes in a way no one else did". A Bristol critic, referring to her performance in the same part, remarked that he couldn't remember a prettier Casilda "than the one Miss Margaret Mitchell makes". While another

Margaret Mitchell as Rose Maybud

critic, having enjoyed her performance as the G&S milkmaid, claimed that "Margaret Mitchell is all virtue as Patience", without being conscious there was any irony in his verdict.

What was she like as a person? Self-assured (obviously) is one answer; cold and hard-boiled is another. But whatever coldness she exhibited towards the world in general was definitely kept under wraps when it came to her attitude towards impressionable males. To put it simply, she fancied, and was determined to get, a clutch of male admirers and didn't mind who knew it; and the feeling was readily reciprocated. Thanks to her looks and figure, she captivated more than a few men in the Company, and sometime during these years she had even married one of them – none other than the chief tenor understudy, previously mentioned: Thomas Hancock.

Hancock, all but five years older than Leonard, and seventeen years older than Margaret herself, has been described as an "easy come, easy go" sort of character, the implication being that he wasn't particularly concerned when she took up with Leonard. It seems plausible to suggest that Leonard was much the more prestigious catch. But what drew *him* to *her*?

The first answer, fairly obviously, was physical attraction; or, as we would put it now, "sex". In the long term, though, there was undoubtedly more to it than that. For, as will be seen in the next couple of chapters, their relationship became, at least on *his* side, one of deep emotional involvement as well.

The two of them were not, it need hardly be said, the first people in D'Oyly Carte to have an affair; and when, where and how their own affair started is now unlikely to be known. But one story Leonard told in later years had a punchline that may have alluded in some way to this aspect of things. The Company were playing *The Gondoliers* in Liverpool and, as Marco, he explained,

> "I knew by experience that, after the arrival of the ducal party in the second act, I was off the stage for just as long as it took to smoke one cigarette. But this was at the time when the Chancellor of the Exchequer had put up the price of cigarettes, and I had given up smoking. Without a cigarette I misjudged the time. Martyn Green, who was playing the Duke of Plaza-Toro, frantically *ad libbed* as the call-boy went in search of me, and I came rushing down the flights of steps from my dressing room three floors up.
>
> Margaret Mitchell was on stage playing Casilda. I asked her: 'Was I missing for long?' She replied: 'Years'."

Meanwhile at the beginning of the 1949-50 tour Leonard had acquired another new part. Near the end of the previous tour Thomas Round had left the Company. Two years earlier, when they were in America, he had been what would now be called headhunted by a film producer. As with the more or less simultaneous approach to Leonard to appear in a Cole Porter show, nothing had come of this. But unlike Leonard, who wanted above all to remain a principal in D'Oyly Carte, and unlike so many other Carte performers down the years

Thomas Round as Frederic
(Photograph: Frederick Sinden)

who were perfectly content to stay as they were, Thomas Round was ambitious. And having now been offered a part in a Johann Strauss-based operetta by a then top impresario, Emile Littler, he jumped at the opportunity to try something different and off he went.

But his departure left a substantial gap in the D'Oyly Carte ranks, and there appeared for the moment to be no one available who was both suitable and ready to fill it. Temporarily at least, two of his parts – Nanki-Poo and Ralph – were given to a chorister, Herbert Newby. Luiz was given to another chorister, Henry Goodier. But that still left Frederic, and Frederic was given to Leonard. It was not, though, a part that really suited him, and in the event he was only to play it for seven months or so when it was given to another chorister, Neville Griffiths.

Still, in semi-exchange for acquiring Frederic, Leonard relinquished the Defendant and Box. But he was now indisputably the Company's senior tenor, the status on which he'd set his sights. "Each season," wrote a Manchester journalist the following March, "seems to enhance his accomplishments."

This, though, is the point at which it's necessary to turn to another aspect of his D'Oyly Carte performing; and it's the one to which the phrase "enhancing his accomplishments" can only be used with qualifications – namely, his recordings.

The recordings in question were the first group of the Company's recordings to be issued as long-players (LPs). They are sometimes referred to as the Decca recordings, sometimes as the Martyn Green/Ella Halman recordings, and even sometimes, because he featured on them all, the Leonard Osborn recordings. They were made between 1949 and 1951, incorporated the whole of the Company's current repertoire except *Cox and Box*, and were done in the following order:

> 1949: *Trial by Jury*; *HMS Pinafore*; *The Pirates of Penzance*
> 1950: *The Mikado*; *The Gondoliers*; *Ruddigore*; *The Yeomen of the Guard*
> 1951: *Iolanthe*; *Patience*

The reason Leonard sang a part on all of them, rather than only on those – admittedly the majority – in which he was appearing or had appeared on stage was the same reason that Thomas Round's place in the Company had yet to be adequately filled: that there seemed for the moment no suitable alternative singer available – though this could hardly be said to be a ringing endorsement. It must also be noted that when it came to the recording of *Patience*, in which he should have sung all the music given to the Duke of Dunstable, he didn't because during the recording period he became unwell. In fact he managed only the four-line verse "Of rite sacrificial" at the beginning of the Act One finale, and the rest of the part was sung at short notice by Neville Griffiths, who by then had stepped into Thomas Round's shoes as the Company's other principal tenor.

This series of recordings, both as a whole and individually, earned many plaudits. A letter published in the *Gramophone* magazine in February 1950, for instance, enthused about the new *Trial by Jury*. "How delighted I was with the performance of all the cast concerned, and also the quality of the recording," the writer declared, before going on to issue an exhortation to the record company: "Don't dally, Decca! I'm yearning for *Yeomen!*"

But these recordings have also come in for their share of criticism, and this, as I indicated in my introduction, is where, all too often, Leonard's name turns up. The following comment on his recorded voice was posted a few years ago on an internet site:

"The Decca series of recordings is marred by Leonard Osborn's tenor ...
By all accounts Osborn was an excellent actor but, regrettably, little of that comes across on record, where his tone sounds particularly nasal and strained."

For myself, I have to say once again that his recordings leave me with mixed feelings, and I *can* understand why so many of those people who know him from his recordings alone are less than impressed. The recordings that come in for the most criticism tend to be his Frederic in *Pirates* and, particularly, his Ralph in *Pinafore*. In neither of these does he seem fully at ease. At times in both of them he is clearly struggling, and in both there is at least one note on which he actually cracks. Each of those cracks cried out for a retake, and the *Pinafore* sequence in which the crack occurred (at the beginning of the Act One finale) was actually given one. But unfortunately the retake was only used for the sets issued as 78s and on EP (extended play) and not, crucially, for the LP issue, which is the issue with which most people will be familiar; and the damage these two recordings have done to Leonard's reputation is incalculable.

His best recordings are, in my view, his Dick Dauntless, the Defendant, Nanki-Poo and – though this may cause some eyebrows to be raised – his Marco in *The Gondoliers*. His rendering of "Take a Pair of sparkling Eyes" may lack the easy fluency of Thomas Round's later recording of the song. But against that, listen to the quiet fun he gets from his verse in "A Regular Royal Queen"; and for me the quartet of young lovers on this recording – himself, Alan Styler, Muriel Harding (Gianetta) and Yvonne Dean (Tessa) – tops the performance of every other quartet, taken as a quartet, who sang the lovers' parts on the various recordings of *The Gondoliers* down the years.

And Leonard's recordings have not lacked other admirers. This is Roger Goodwin:

"As someone who never saw him on stage, my impressions of his singing are in opposition to one another, but as a trained singer myself, I appreciate his vocal qualities:
    Strident but sensitive.
    Wayward tone but characterful.
    Vowels distorted but diction clear.
    His voice production is mainly sound but flawed. Breath control is suspect. Sustained notes lack support from the diaphragm.

But the overall result is human, attractive and memorable. Very strange!"

This is Bruce Doery, who did see him on stage – even though only once, as Fairfax – and who has this to say:

"For me he was a great favourite. My introduction to G&S was largely through the Decca recordings on which he featured.
Unfortunately I am unable to recall much of that Fairfax performance except, perhaps, his entrance with the dialogue leading up to 'Is Life a Boon?' He was all I had expected from his recordings and photos I had seen."

And this is Katie Barnes who, like Roger Goodwin, never saw him on stage even once, and who has also, therefore, formed an assessment of him as a singer from his recordings alone:

"You have only to listen to those recordings to feel the charm rolling over you in waves, personality to knock you cold at ten paces. And that voice! No wonder female fans collapsed, metaphorically speaking, at his feet."

Which, as a recommendation of those recordings, could hardly be bettered. And even his singing of Ralph has had its admirers. Referring to the recordings of *Trial by Jury* and *HMS Pinafore* jointly, a reviewer in the *Gramophone* wrote:

"The honours go, in the first place, to Miss Harding as the Plaintiff and Josephine, and to Mr Osborn as the Defendant and Ralph Rackstraw."

Pass! Yet as a final word on the subject, I can only repeat another point I made earlier: that even at its best, his recorded voice gives only a hint of the impact he made on stage – in person – in the theatre; that to fully appreciate Leonard Osborn as a performer, he had to be seen, not just heard.

From the performing point of view the 1949-50 tour had no special highlights. But it was a different matter with the tour after that. For on that tour – the tour of 1950-51 – there were two. The first of these, extending from October to February – was another D'Oyly Carte visit to America.

Looked at overall, this latest visit was less successful than its 1947-48 predecessor. True, it took in ten venues (plus Toronto in Canada) as against just two on the former occasion. But the itinerary was badly arranged. On each of their previous visits they had opened to maximum publicity and enthusiasm in New York, whereas this time they began in New Haven in Connecticut, which had no hope of competing with New York in terms of glamour, and took in other less glamorous venues along the way. As Martyn Green put it in his autobiography, "it was like going into America through the back door", and in some towns business was so bad that at one time the management even contemplated aborting the visit early. But at length things perked up; and by the time they finally reached New York for their last four weeks in the country, the enthusiasm was as great as ever.

Nor had things been initially helped by the current international situation. The visit took place against the backdrop of the Korean War, which had broken out that summer – another war so soon after the end of World War II; another war in which America was heavily involved.

But out of this came at least *some* positive good. New York in particular needed a diversion to take its mind off the war, and D'Oyly Carte in Gilbert and Sullivan – D'Oyly Carte on form – provided exactly the diversion that fitted the bill. With the Company's arrival in the city, declared the *New York Times*, life seemed "not quite so grim as it was before".

The Company brought with them the same repertoire they had brought on the previous visit with the exception of *The Yeomen of the Guard*. More surprisingly, they had also chosen not to bring the newly revived *Ruddigore*. So that left Leonard with just three major parts to play on the visit. But his spell as Frederic having come to an end, he was also playing Box and the Defendant once more. And it was after the first of his performances as the Defendant in New York that he received the following fan letter from someone with whom he was apparently on familiar terms:

"Dear Leonard

It did me good to pick up the *New York World Telegram* and read words of praise regarding you in *Trial by Jury* in Manhattan. I saw the review, headed 'Savoyards Treated to Twin Bill', so I hastily read it, hoping to find mention of yourself.

There it was: a printed applause for your splendid voice, which goes to prove I was entirely right when I recognised your vast ability.

This is merely a note of remembrance and to wish you continued success.

Most cordially
George [Browning]"

And when on February 24th (1951) the New York season ended, certain members of the Company felt almost as sad about leaving as the New Yorkers were sad to see them go. But there was no way their return home could be delayed now, for they had another high profile engagement – the second highlight of that performing year – to fulfil.

It was now summer, the summer of the Festival of Britain, that countrywide celebration of British achievements and endeavours. In such a festival it seemed only right that Gilbert and Sullivan should have their place – and D'Oyly Carte duly gave them that place with a thirteen week season at the operas' titular home, the Savoy. It was the first time the Company had played the Savoy for ten years. It was also the first time that Leonard, along with all but a few of the other performers involved, had played the Savoy at all.

The season opened on May 7th with a rousing performance of *The Mikado* on stage and the unmistakable figure of Winston Churchill in the theatre box; and the season was a triumph from first to last. Even so, it's possible that for some of the Company members themselves, the most memorable occasion during those thirteen weeks occurred not at the Savoy itself but at the Theatre Royal, Drury Lane. For there on July 9th, as a contribution to a star-studded "late night" programme – the stars including Sybil Thorndike and Alec Clunes – they presented a sequence from Act Two of *The Gondoliers*, beginning with the chorus "With Ducal Pomp". And Leonard duly came on as Marco at the appropriate moment. No missed entrance panic for him *that* night.

The season was rounded off on August 4th with a "surprise" programme – the first D'Oyly Carte surprise "Last Night" since the early 1930s. On this occasion the items performed were Act One of *The Gondoliers* and Act Two of *The Mikado*, which meant that Leonard signed off for the season embarking (so to speak) for Barataria.

But the end of the season, it had been known for some weeks, was to be more than the end of the season full stop. For that summer, in what can only be described as a mass exodus, more than half the performers who took part in the Savoy performances were leaving the Company. It was the biggest single exodus of performers in D'Oyly Carte history.

And it was also the end of a D'Oyly Carte era. The immediate post-war era. The era that had seen the return to the Company of Martyn Green. And Leonard.

Leonard with golf bag at a stage door

54

"Bruising and Sprains", 1951-53

The fact that so many people had left the Company all at once hardly seemed to augur well for the D'Oyly Carte future. How could it have been otherwise? Those who left were mostly reticent about their reasons for going, or at least were reticent publicly; and this being 1951 rather than, say, 1991 or 2001, they were not hounded by headline-hunting journalists into abandoning that reticence. Not all of them, of course, left for the same reason. But, broadly speaking, the majority of them left because of general dissatisfaction with the way they'd been treated by the Company management, along with disputes about money.

So who *were* the people who had left? Four names especially stand out, and top of the list has to be Martyn Green. Martyn Green had been described by one American critic back in 1948 as a performer who could "do no wrong as far as loyal Savoyards are concerned". Not only that, but he was "well nigh perfect most of the time", and he was obviously going to be, in the modern phrase, a hard act to follow.

Second on the list, both for her personal popularity and the robust style of her performances, must come Ella Halman. Third comes Richard Watson, who had replaced his near-namesake Richard Walker as principal heavy baritone in 1948, as fruity-voiced a Pooh-Bah, Don Alhambra *et al* as there has probably ever been.

And fourth there was Margaret Mitchell, taking her leave after seven years, which was a reasonable length of stay for a young soprano. According to her Company record card, she had written to the management during the Savoy season "saying that she did not wish to continue", and it was "understood that she had accepted [an] offer for a film in America". Nothing, however, came of this in the end, and instead she was taken on by the comedian and musician Vic Oliver whose touring show needed a glamour girl; and Leonard later told Frederick Sinden that "she was offered more money by him than she'd ever had with D'Oyly Carte".

So Margaret had gone. Margaret was no longer around. But Leonard wasn't part of the exodus. Leonard, at least for the moment, stayed on. Yet this didn't stop their affair continuing, even if with their different touring schedules they were now apart more often than they were together. So who among the previous set of principals stayed on with him?

The leading figure here was undoubtedly Darrell Fancourt, now into his fourth decade in the Company. There was Alan Styler, he of the abundant confidence and the smoking. There was Muriel Harding, Gianetta (as on the recording) to Leonard's Marco, Elsie (similarly) to his Fairfax, and previously Mabel (similarly again) to his Frederic; and there was Neville Griffiths, the second principal tenor. These four, along with Leonard himself and the sprinkling of more experienced choristers who were still around, provided a leavening of continuity that at the start of the new (1951-52) tour was little short of crucial.

For the departure of so many of the old hands had necessitated the taking on of an equivalent number of newcomers, and those newcomers had to be trained and rehearsed – rehearsed again and again – and it fell to the remaining old hands to show the way forward. And not only the old hands on stage. Just as important were two other figures responsible for the productions as a whole. One of these was the Stage Director, who since April 1949 had been Darrell Fancourt's wife, Eleanor Evans.

And the other was a man it was too easy to take for granted because he was always there, always reliable, always in control, always conveying the sense that everything was all right: Isidore Godfrey, the Musical Director, who had been with D'Oyly Carte since 1925. Some months before the post-Savoy exodus a journalist in America, where he was far less taken for granted than he sometimes was in Britain, had vividly described how much it meant to have him there, performance after performance, in the orchestra pit:

> "Mr Godfrey ... well, Mr Godfrey still is quite a conductor. He opens the score but doesn't look at it. He keeps his desk light down so it doesn't blind down front sitters. He works with affection and the kind of skill that always reminds me I have forgotten too much of the charm, wit and talent of [the Gilbert and Sullivan] collaboration."

So with all that was involved, the run up to and first weeks and months of the new tour were a time of immensely hard work for the newcomers and the old hands in the Company alike, Leonard naturally among them. But – and it wasn't long before, in his own case, he decided there was a definite "but" – he very much got the feeling he was being put upon by the management. And on September 27th, just ten days after the new tour began, he wrote another letter setting out his complaints.

It was a letter not dissimilar in subject matter to the letter he had written to Rupert D'Oyly Carte prior to the 1947-48 American visit (see pages 31-2). In that letter he had asked to be given more to do. But this time his driving force was the reverse. This time he was protesting he was being asked to do more than he'd agreed to do, and this time "protesting" was very much the word. In addition, it need hardly be said, he was writing not to Rupert D'Oyly Carte but to Bridget:

"Dear Miss Carte

I thank you for your letter of the 25th September.

From the tone of your letter it is apparent that I have been misrepresented – or misunderstood – and it is for that reason I wish to have the position cleared up now.

When I had my interview with you in June 1950, the casting for the tenor roles at the time was as under:

Ruddigore,Yeomen,Gondoliers,Iolanthe, Patience:	Osborn
Pirates:	Griffiths
Pinafore, Mikado, Trial:	Newby
Cox and Box:	Hancock

At that interview you suggested that maybe I needed a rest from so many operas; that *Ruddigore* and *Yeomen* would not be taken to America; and that Mr Griffiths would be playing the three favourite American operas, *Mikado*, *Pinafore* and *Pirates*, but would I once again play Defendant and *Cox and Box* – just for the American tour. Later it was found more convenient for me to play those small parts for the seven weeks prior to the American tour, and I have your letter confirming this arrangement – i.e. I should be playing the five roles for those seven weeks, as previously, plus Defendant and Box – in spite of my apparent tiredness!!

Whilst we were in America, Mr Nightingale approached me in Springfield, and asked me if I would play the two small parts in question for the Festival Season at the Savoy, and that was also agreed between us.

In July of this year Mr Nightingale told me of your offer for the new tour, and I mentioned particularly these two parts; that when they were once more back in the repertory I did not expect to play them in the provinces; and I pointed out that I had taken them over only for the American and Savoy seasons. I was assured that 'That'll be all right'. When I received my contract for this tour I was under the impression that this point had been raised with you.

True, these roles are for only half an hour, and I have the rest of the evening off, but contrary to popular belief they are not 'romps' and 'almost like a night off'. They carry as much responsibility as any of the bigger roles, and I work just as hard in that half hour.

All of the foregoing was explained to Mr Worsley [Bruce Worsley, successor to Hugh Jones as D'Oyly Carte Business Manager] last week in Dudley, when he asked me whether my Defendant costume fitted me. It was also pointed out that if I was required for Defendant and Box, I should be free only when *Mikado* is played.

It would appear that this latter point has been seized upon as suggesting that I 'feel I shall have too much work to do'. That suggestion originated in your office in June 1950 when I was playing five of the eight main tenor roles, a suggestion with which I still disagree.

The role of Defendant has always been a tenor understudy part until I took it over under special circumstances; and at present there is in the Company an understudy – Mr Newby – who has played it for a year.

I am prepared to carry on with [the two parts] until after the Scottish visit [Glasgow and Edinburgh, October 1st – November 3rd] for I appreciate the amount of work that still has to be done with a practically new Company.

As to your last paragraph, if you feel you have to relieve me of my position, I should like to know as soon as possible, so that I can make further arrangements."

No copy of Bridget's letter that prompted this response seems to have survived. Consequently it's impossible to be sure how the apparent misunderstandings took hold and who, if anyone, was to blame for them. Unusually with a Leonard letter, it's not entirely clear what he was trying to say. Did he or did he not feel at some stage that he had too much to do? Moreover on one point of fact he was definitely wrong: as mentioned earlier in this book, the Defendant had not always been previously treated as an understudy part.

And what of that sentence about Bridget possibly relieving him of his position? If she did include a remark which suggested this, she almost certainly hadn't expected it to be interpreted that way. For on October 3rd Frederic Lloyd, who had just taken over from Alfred Nightingale as General Manager of the Company (the senior position after herself) wrote to him on her behalf in terms that indicated a clear, even urgent, desire to mollify him and sort things out:

"Dear Mr Osborn (*wrote Lloyd*)

I am replying to your letter of the 27th September written to Miss D'Oyly Carte, and I think the whole situation has been misunderstood.

Miss D'Oyly Carte felt that you were being overworked, but in the circumstances it has been rather difficult with so many new members to fill the various parts adequately.

The last paragraph of her letter of the 25th September was not in any way intended to mean that we were going to relieve you of your position, but that we should try and help you in order that you might have a little more time for rest.

It is only too easy to misinterpret what is sometimes put down on paper, and as I propose to visit the Company before very long, I think it would be an excellent plan if you and I could meet and talk this matter over, when I am sure that we can solve the whole situation satisfactorily."

Frederic Lloyd himself, a figure who was to play a prominent part in Leonard's life from then on, came from an ecclesiastical family. Previously he had worked for CEMA – the Council for Education and Music in the Arts, and the precursor of the Arts Council – and had also been an organising director of the Festival of Britain. Born about 1918, he was very much of Leonard's generation. A tall, patrician figure, he had acquired the politician's or bureaucrat's knack of appearing, whether in writing or speech, to say more – or give out more information - than he actually did. His main concern at pretty well all times was to keep Bridget happy without in the process, if he could help it, upsetting anybody else; and he was particularly adept at dampening down any controversies connected with, or conflicts within, the Company that happened to raise their unwelcome heads.

But he was, or became, a genuine lover of G&S. And while, during what were to prove his many years at the helm, he didn't take to every member of the Company who was on the books during those years, he appears in general to have approved of Leonard and to have treated him with consideration and courtesy. Certainly on this occasion his intervention had the necessary effect. Leonard accepted his assurance that he was under no threat, and he also had his wish with regard to the two curtain-raisers. By mid-December he had played the Defendant and Box for the last time.

So was he (Leonard) justified in getting wound up and tetchy over the way he thought he was being treated at this time? The answer is probably less important than the fact that he got wound up at the time he did, and may well have had less to do with his workload in the Company than what was happening in his life outside it. In other words, it's back to his affair with Margaret Mitchell.

At some point around this time Margaret Mitchell and Thomas Hancock separated and eventually divorced. It was an amicable separation; they each simply agreed to go their own way. Leonard, meanwhile, was still married; and, not surprisingly, the affair was now causing ructions and turmoil at home. Along with a fear that he might be pushed out of D'Oyly Carte was a tormenting feeling that he might have to go anyway.

This had first become apparent during the Savoy season when, in another letter to Bridget, he had written that he might have to terminate his engagement himself. Then, to confuse the issue, had come the long letter quoted above; and the following June Frederic Lloyd was reporting that while Leonard had signed his contract for the next (1952-53) tour, he had asked to have a three months' option inserted. The reason for this was stark: that "he may be faced with domestic trouble", and that if this proved to be the case, he thought it would not only be embarrassing for himself but for the whole Company, and that it was "wiser for all concerned if he was in a position to leave at a three months' notice". As regards the Company this turned out a false alarm, an option he never took up. But the domestic trouble itself was not stilled, and eventually he and his wife also separated.

None of this, however, seems to have affected his performances on stage any more than his previous drop in self-confidence had affected them. Here are just a couple of his notices from this time, both of them eulogising:

"As Colonel Fairfax … Leonard Osborn was dashing, handsome and had a fine voice."

(*Brighton Gazette*, June 1952)

"Audiences are, of course, made up of young and old, and I direct this comment to the former. Hollywood could not wish for a more winsome heart-throb than Leonard Osborn as Dick Dauntless"

(*Bristol Evening Post*, May 1953)

even at the age of thirty-eight!

And if his private troubles didn't affect his performances on stage, they also didn't prevent him continuing to present a smiling face to his fans at the stage door. With most people he kept quiet about his problems – this was still, after all, the era of the stiff upper lip – and managed not to let them sour the atmosphere within the Company itself.

Thinking back over his many years in D'Oyly Carte, Darrell Fancourt described the current, post-Martyn Green team as the happiest he'd known in all that time. The mass exodus of 1951, however damaging to the Company's future it had seemed at the time, turned out before long to have brought huge benefits.

For the arrival of so many new and, above all, fresh and youthful faces acted as a positive rejuvenation, bringing with them as they did a sense of spontaneity, of vigour and zest for their work that was not weighed down by any baggage from the past. And their effect on things was immediate. By the end of their first (1951-52) tour Graham Davis, the editor of the *Gilbert & Sullivan Journal*, was claiming that not only had their performances reached "a high level of excellence" within a matter of weeks, but that by the tour's end they had "soared to inspired heights of all but perfection". And even if that was an exaggeration, it indicated – at the very least – that things were moving in the right direction. It was as though the austere and difficult years that followed the end of the war were over at last.

So who were the new, youthful Company members who now joined Fancourt, Leonard, Alan Styler, Muriel Harding and Neville Griffiths as the new set of principals? Again there are four names that call for special mention. And the first of these names is that of Peter Pratt, who replaced Martyn Green as the Company's principal comedian.

Peter Pratt, though, was not a new name in the Company itself. He had joined as a chorister in 1945 and in due course had become Green's understudy. But he could certainly be said to be youthful – a mere twenty-eight when he took over. (Green by contrast had been thirty-five when he took over from Henry Lytton.) And though following Green presented him with a huge challenge, it was a challenge he surmounted with remarkable speed.

Thus as early as April 1952 a Bristol critic, writing of his performance as the Duke of Plaza-Toro, was moved to suggest that "if the evidence on this occasion was reliable, it [seems] as if Mr Pratt might reach a maturity of style a good deal quicker than did some of his distinguished predecessors". He was "a first rate singer," wrote another critic three years later, and "a performer who is never dazzled with his own cleverness". Much later still, Leonard himself was to describe him as "a worker" who was in essence a character actor rather than being a comedian or "funny man" as such, but who nevertheless got the comedy of his parts across to excellent effect.

The second person to mention here is Ann Drummond-Grant, who could be considered a new name even though in a sense she wasn't new at all, and was some way past being called youthful in anyone's language. She had been in D'Oyly Carte for a number of years in the 1930s, and in fact had overlapped with Leonard in his first year and more in the Company as a chorister. At that time she had been a soprano. But since then two things had happened: she had married Isidore Godfrey and her voice had deepened. She had now returned in place of Ella Halman as principal contralto, and in due course acquired the universally adopted nickname "Drummie".

Third on the list is Fisher Morgan (Thomas Fisher Morgan, to give him his full name) who replaced Richard Watson as heavy baritone. Unlike, say, Peter Pratt, Alan Styler and, indeed, Leonard himself, Fisher Morgan had been appointed directly as a principal; and at forty-three, as he then was, he was another who could scarcely be described as youthful. Solidly built, he comfortably fitted the heavy baritone mould both in a physical sense and the way he portrayed his various characters. His performance as Don Alhambra, for example, was described by one critic as "the quintessence of restrained and slumbering comedy".

The fourth name here is that of Shirley Hall. Shirley Hall was the soprano who replaced Margaret Mitchell. With a background in repertory theatre and revue, she was another performer who came in as a principal. She also came into the youthful category and she obviously had talent. "Shirley Hall's lovely, effortless voice, a radiant light on any ensemble it joins, was a paramount joy in this performance, and it will surely prove to be an outstanding memory of the whole week," wrote a Harrogate reporter, cheerfully mixing his metaphors, of her Casilda in January 1952. But however brightly her light may have shone during that week or any other week of that tour, it was to shine on D'Oyly Carte audiences for a relatively short time thereafter. She left the Company at the beginning of 1953.

So much for the newcomers. But there is one of the other principals – one of the survivors from the previous years – who also needs special mention here. That other principal is Neville Griffiths.

Neville Griffiths, then in his late twenties, had joined the Company in April 1949. Like Leonard he had been in the RAF. Like Leonard, too, he had started as a chorister. But he had been marked out as a potential principal from the first, and as the Company's two leading tenors he and Leonard made an interesting pair. Unlike the previous pairing of Leonard and Thomas Round, though, Leonard and Neville Griffiths could not have been more different.

Short and stocky, and with a certain boyishness in both manner and looks, Neville Griffiths was never going to attract legions of adoring female fans in the way the other two did. He was never going to be a matinee idol. His promotion was primarily due to his singing voice, which was strong, rich-toned and, above all, reliable. It also owed a lot to his origins.

Griffiths had been born in South Wales, and had been a member of his local male voice choir. He was one of a number of Welsh-born performers who joined D'Oyly Carte down the years (Fisher Morgan being another). His Welshness was always a distinctive part of him, and his voice always retained

Neville Griffiths as Nanki-Poo

its Welsh lilt. "Mr Griffiths was singing Nanki-Poo in a beautiful Welsh tenor," enthused a Chicago critic during the 1950–51 American tour.

A good team player with an affable, friendly personality, he was universally liked. A "very nice person and popular in the Company," says his Company record. Like Thomas Round he gave the impression of a man at ease with himself; and he also had a quiet sense of fun. There was to be an occasion in 1958 during a performance of *The Gondoliers* when he caused much amusement among the men's chorus by quietly singing a risqué comic song inWelsh that exactly fitted the G&S strains they were singing themselves. Who said D'Oyly Carte was staid?

Since August 1950 Griffiths had been playing three of the tenor leads, Frederic, Nanki-Poo and Ralph, the last two of which he had taken over from Herbert Newby, who had reverted to being just a chorister and small part player. When contrasted with Leonard's workload, though, three parts in a repertoire of eight full-length operas and two curtain-raisers hardly counted as equality.

And this was reflected in their respective pay packets. Leonard had been given another pay rise for the 1950-51 tour, taking him from thirty-five pounds a week to thirty-seven pounds ten shillings. Admittedly for the 1951-52 tour he had not received any further rise – the first time no annual rise had been forthcoming since he'd rejoined the Company. But his thirty-seven pounds ten still compared favourably with the twenty-five pounds received for that tour by Griffiths, and he continued without question to be the Company's senior tenor.

It's worth noting, too, that once Griffiths had been promoted from the chorus, the paths of the two of them never crossed on stage. The only operas then in the repertoire that could at a pinch accommodate two principal tenors were *The Yeomen of the Guard* and *The Gondoliers*. But while Leonard continued to play the chief tenor lead in both of these – Fairfax and Marco – Griffiths never played either of the other parts – Leonard Meryll and Luiz – on stage, though he did sing Leonard Meryll on the *Yeomen* Decca recording.

So, in the manner of Cox and Box, the two only saw each other when, as it were, they passed on the stairs. But, that said, they always got on well together. Perhaps because as performers they were very different, there was no rivalry between them; and Elizabeth Howarth, a chorister Griffiths married in 1953, speaks of Leonard with real warmth. All of which leads conveniently to another point and a point that can best be put as a question: what did some of the *rest* of his colleagues think about him?

In terms of him as a performer, the answer is clear. There may have been the odd exception, because in life there always is, but overall the feeling was near-unanimous: a feeling of immense admiration, lessened only by the equally widespread acceptance of the fact that his singing voice was sometimes suspect. Darrell Fancourt's opinion of his Dick Dauntless has already been mentioned. Another unashamed admirer was Cynthia Morey, who joined the Company as a chorister in 1951 and later became a principal soprano. "Tenors in the D'Oyly Carte Opera Company," she has written, "came and went down the years. Some made more of a mark than others. Leonard in my opinion features larger than most. I would unhesitatingly place a large star by his name." He was a "master of characterisation".

Then there is Trevor Hills, a baritone who also joined the Company as a chorister in 1951 and became understudy to Fisher Morgan, and who thought Leonard "excellent" in his parts. There is Frederick Sinden, who describes him as "a consummate artist". There is Jeffrey Skitch who in 1952 joined as understudy to Alan Styler, and who thought him in particular "a very good mover and an excellent dancer". And there is Jon Ellison, who in 1953 also joined as a baritone chorister, and who describes his performances in still more glowing terms. Leonard, he says, had "a really great stage presence and a dignity that he never let slip.

"When he made an entrance I always felt that his whole attitude was complete confidence, and that the stage was his to use to the best advantage.

Whilst saying this, however, I do not mean that he was a selfish performer at all, for he also had the ability to remain perfectly still, yet stay very much within the action when someone else had centre stage."

But in terms of the way his colleagues saw him as a *person*, their views varied considerably, and in certain cases were definitely not so favourable. On the one hand Cynthia Morey saw him as "always charming, never ruffled or bad tempered", while Frederick Sinden describes him as "quite the gentleman".

Yet against that, certain of the other male choristers were much less impressed. He was never really, in the modern phrase, a "people person". Both Trevor Hills and Jon Ellison suggest he could come across as aloof, and Hills says "rather offhand" too. He had a habit of addressing them and their fellows as "Laddie", a habit that could be irritating and also sound patronising; a way of pointing out that he was a principal and they were not. But as with that other aloof figure, Rupert D'Oyly Carte, his offhandedness and apparent hauteur were almost certainly a cover for shyness and, in his own case, insecurity. Jeffrey Skitch sums up the unfortunate effect this could have, and not only among the choristers: "One felt a slight unease in his company."

Along with this must be mentioned an inability, as Frederick Sinden puts it, to suffer fools gladly – Barry Pendry, the graphologist, spotted this too; and he was good – sometimes too good – at delivering a frosty put-down. There was one occasion, for example – this is Sinden again – when he responded in this way to a newish chorister, an uncouth, scruffily dressed individual (so hardly a chorister of the normal D'Oyly Carte type) who had previously worked the music halls. Lounging around somewhere, the latter pulled out a cigarette and, catching sight of Leonard nearby, called out to him: "Got a light, chum?" Leonard turned towards him with a glare and said icily: "I have *not* got a light and I am not your chum."

And if he didn't get ruffled and didn't lose his temper overall, there was nonetheless one occasion when he lost it well and truly. The details this time come from Jon Ellison:

"We were playing the New Theatre, Oxford, having the previous two weeks played the Theatre Royal, Birmingham. I think it was a Wednesday matinee, and I was sitting getting made up in the gents' chorus room when, amidst all the babble of chatter, the door burst open and in stormed Leonard with his face ... I think 'incandescent' would be a fair description, such was his anger.

His opening words – I recall them as if it were yesterday – were 'Who is responsible for this?' and he held aloft what appeared to be a letter.

It appeared that one of the gents' chorus had indulged in a torrid love affair with a young lady in Birmingham during the previous two weeks, and had told her his name was Leonard Osborn.

The said young lady had written a most revealing and passionate letter, saying what a wonderful time she had experienced and could hardly wait for an encore.

The perpetrator was never revealed, though a couple of names were suggested."

"I can report," Ellison concludes, "that Leonard did eventually calm down, and I was told that in time he saw the funny side of it." It was, after all, a considerable compliment in its way.

Not always commented on, though as important as any of the above, was the often considerate and kindly side of Leonard's nature. In particular he would willingly offer help and advice to any of his colleagues who approached him with concerns about their performances. Right from the start of his D'Oyly Carte days he had given considerable thought not only to his own parts but to G&S as a whole; and he was always willing to pass on the results of his thinking.

Someone who especially benefited from this willingness was Frederick Sinden to whom, on the quiet (there could have been trouble if the management had got to hear about it) he gave much sound guidance and several useful tips in connection with the parts – Fairfax, Marco and Dick Dauntless – in which Sinden was understudying him. Another member of the Company who benefited similarly from his guidance was Sinden's wife, Beryl Dixon, who was then understudy to the principal soubrette, Joyce Wright, and whom he quietly coached in a number of her roles.

Jeffrey Skitch, too, has a memory that chimes in with all this:

"Once at Golders Green Hippodrome after I had been with the Company a fairly short time" (*he says*) "Alan Styler, who should have been playing Giuseppe, was off, and I had to go on for him at just a few hours notice. I had my first rehearsal in the part on the morning of the show. Leonard, who was playing Marco, was extremely helpful to me throughout a nerve-wracking evening – and I needed all the help I could get!"

If that was an evening on which Leonard was able to help a fellow performer, there was an evening during the next (1952-53) tour when he was the one who needed help.

Should you ask anybody who knew or saw Leonard Osborn during his years as a D'Oyly Carte performer what he or she remembers *most* about him, you will probably get told three things. First, as likely as not and as already indicated, will be a lauding of his Dick Dauntless. Second, or possibly third, will be a comment on his singing voice. And third, or possibly even second, will be a reference to his "accident".

It was January 1953. The Company were playing the Memorial Theatre at Stratford-upon-Avon. On Monday January 13th they performed *Ruddigore*, and the lady reviewing the production for the *Stratford-upon-Avon Herald* was unstinting in her praise:

> "The Company is at its best in *Ruddigore*. Darrell Fancourt is so superb as the ghostly Sir Roderic and sings 'The Ghosts' High Noon' with such authority and power that it is doubly hard to forgive Gilbert for bringing him back to cursed life.
>
> Sir Ruthven [Robin Oakapple] is one of Peter Pratt's best performances. And Leonard Osborn's Richard Dauntless is notable for good singing and really nautically light and nimble feet in the hornpipe."

But she wouldn't have couched her assessment of Leonard in quite those terms had she instead been present at *Ruddigore's* second performance on the Tuesday. There he was, that Tuesday evening, making his first entrance – the spectacular first entrance when he would leap over the railing. On this occasion, however, as he made to grasp the particular point of the railing he always earmarked for this, his hand slipped, he caught his foot in one of the fishing nets draped *across* the railing and fell headlong on to the main part of the stage below. Somehow he got to his feet again and, though obviously dazed, injured and in great pain, he managed to sing his opening song and even to dance his usual hornpipe.

But that was *all* he could manage. After finishing the hornpipe, instead of carrying on with the dialogue that follows, he got himself into the wings and there he collapsed.

Meanwhile behind the scenes, a number of people had realised what had happened, and immediately there was frantic activity. Clearly he could not go on with his performance; Frederick Sinden as his understudy must go on in his place. Sinden, though, was already dressed for his own eventual entrance as one of the *Ruddigore* "bucks and blades". But now, accompanied and urged on by Peter Pratt, he dashed back up to his dressing room, flung off his chorus costume, donned his costume for Dauntless, effected corresponding alterations to his make-up and, despite one or two other people flapping around and getting in the way, was there in the wings ready to go on as Leonard came off.

But what were the injuries Leonard sustained? You can take your choice from the suggestions that have been put forward: a broken ankle, a chipped bone in his arm and damage to his shoulder and chin, a couple of cracked ribs, a cracked elbow – the last two of these being what, much later, he himself claimed his injuries to have been – and he should have known what they'd been if anyone did.

Leonard as Dick Dauntless with Peter Pratt as Robin Oakapple
(Photograph: Houston Rogers)

Yet that can only be described as a story that developed in the telling. Fortunately – remarkably – he got off far more lightly than any or all of this might suggest. He had immediately been taken to the local hospital and two days later the doctor who saw him reported that "x-ray examination revealed no fractures, and I think his injuries are confined to bruising and sprains". In consequence "I expect the period of his incapacity from professional work [will] be from ten-fourteen days", and would probably be even less if he could be given "some massage, etc.".

And so it proved when at Blackpool, precisely ten days after that report was penned, he stepped on stage again as Fairfax, while his first Dauntless after the accident came on February 3rd, just eight days after that. Nonetheless the recovery process as a whole took considerably longer than the period he was off work. The following letter, another of his letters to Bridget D'Oyly Carte, was written almost six months later:

"Dear Miss Carte

I spoke to Mr Lloyd yesterday about the outcome of the claim for my accident that Equity were making on my behalf, and he has asked me to write and let you know the facts.

It appears that Equity have had second thoughts about the claim, on the advice of the solicitor that 'we cannot rate the chances of success in a claim other than very moderate'. This advice was placed before Equity's Executive Committee last week, and they decided not to grant me legal protection in the claim. They add that if I care to pursue the claim, then I have to do so on my own account, and bear my own costs if it fails.

I have been given to understand that the probable failure of the claim rests on the fact that negligence on the part of the Company cannot be proved.

As you know, my salary was stopped for the eleven performances I was off – a loss of income of fifty-eight pounds eighteen shillings and sevenpence, and the cost of treatment was sixty-five guineas. The reason this is rather high is that I had about three hours treatment a day to get me back to work quickly. Also the treatment was continued for about five weeks afterwards on my days off, and at weekends.

I had hoped that this claim would have been settled before the end of the tour, but now I have the bill for treatment to settle myself, with the prospect of seven weeks with no pay ahead of me.

I should be grateful if you could see your way towards helping me in this matter."

And as she had done when Arnold Smith's bill for sorting out his vocal problems had come in four years earlier, Bridget paid up; and despite the fact that the Cartes always had a reputation for financial tightness, did so neither grudgingly nor just in part as Leonard had more or less requested, but in full – and promptly.

But what had caused the accident in the first place? Why had it occurred the night it did, rather than any other night? Leonard always made a point of asking the "props" man to leave a gap in the fishing nets through which he could grasp the railing and vault it unencumbered, and after the event there was speculation that one of the girls' chorus had inadvertently, and without him realising, spread some of the netting over the gap.

This may have been the case, or it may not. But even if it *was* the case, it was unlikely to have been more than a contributory factor to what happened, not its prime cause. Far more likely, the prime cause had to do with his state of mind.

It was a few days earlier – or even the day before – or possibly even the day of the accident itself. Leonard had gone to the theatre to pick up the post that had come for him that morning. Having done so, he shortly afterwards caught sight of Frederick Sinden. "Freddie," he said, "come and have coffee with me. I've had some awful news."

The two of them sat together on the theatre terrace. Leonard had a letter in his hand. He indicated it now, jerking the words out bleakly as he spoke.

"This letter. It's from Maggie – Maggie Mitchell. She says, 'Sorry, it – it's all off between us.' Freddie, she's turned me down!" Then suddenly, in desolation, he gave way to a flood of tears.

And that letter, and what was in it, surely explains everything. He could put on a smiling face in public, because the ability to smile in public whatever the circumstances is a near-essential for any public performer. But in the hours and days that followed the letter's arrival part of his mind was clearly elsewhere. And when part of a person's mind is elsewhere, isn't that so often when accidents happen?

If *Ruddigore* was the opera that gave Leonard his nastiest and most painful stage experience, it also, on another occasion, provided him with what was potentially his most embarrassing one.

It was the scene between Dick Dauntless and Robin Oakapple that immediately follows the hornpipe. At the line "Will you do this thing for me? Can you, do you think?" Peter Pratt as Oakapple pretended as usual to check Dauntless's pulse with the aid of a large old watch, which he would deliberately shake hard. On this occasion when he shook it, though, it broke and fell to pieces at his feet. Leonard bent to pick the pieces up, and as he did so the back of his trousers split, and "his ensuing ten agonised minutes on the stage demanded" (as it was delicately put) "great restraint in attitude and movement".

The D'Oyly Carte performers in each decade of the Company's history were famous. Not to the extent that prime ministers, film stars and sporting heroes are famous, but famous in their own limited sphere. As Peter Pratt was to put it in an interview in 1959: "Most leading artists are known to millions. I suppose I am known to about a hundred thousand – those, I mean, who know me as a person." But among those hundred thousand were any number of people – fans - who were loyal and enthusiastic in the extreme; people who wanted nothing so much as to develop a bond with him and (or) other members of the Company not just at the stage door but away from the theatre too.

One result of this was that many in the Company – mainly, though not entirely, the principals – found themselves invited to be celebrity guests at this or that function on this or that occasion. Not all of them, admittedly, could take equal advantage of such invitations. It depended at least to some extent on how many of the operas a particular performer was playing in at a particular time. Peter Pratt and Ann Drummond-Grant, for instance – as indeed every member of the chorus – played in all of them, and consequently had little time to spare for outside activities of this nature.

But where Leonard was concerned it was rather different. For never having been in *The Mikado*, which was rarely off the bill for long, and now not being required on *Cox and Box* and *Trial by Jury* nights either, he could reckon on two or three free evenings most weeks.

The earliest celebrity-type invitation that came his way is impossible to establish for certain, but may have been one he received in October or November 1947 from the headmaster of his old school. The school was approaching its twenty first birthday. Would he come along and sing at the celebration that was being held to mark the occasion? He duly wrote to Rupert D'Oyly Carte requesting permission from him to travel down to London to do so; the Company would then be playing Manchester, so it would mean quite a jaunt. Nonetheless, as the evening in question was one on which they'd be performing *The Mikado*, for which he wouldn't be needed, it seems likely his request was granted.

In April 1952 he gave a short talk on the G&S "tradition" to a party of overseas students in Bristol, concentrating particularly on *The Mikado*, a performance of which they were being taken to see immediately afterwards. The following year he gave a talk to an equivalent audience again, and a few months after that he gave a talk to the Cardiff Gramophone Society.

But the largest number of invitations he received to speak or perform came, as they did for other members of the Company, from branches of the Gilbert and Sullivan Society. The *Gilbert & Sullivan Journal* of May 1950 included a description of an evening's entertainment he and Muriel Harding had given to the Liverpool branch of the Society that March:

> "Their programme consisted of eleven items from no less than eight of the operas [and] Mr Osborn made it all the more interesting, particularly for those members who are not too familiar with the operas, by prefacing each item with a brief account of the dramatic situation where the particular song or duet occurs …
>
> The last half hour was given over to community singing, enthusiastically led by Miss Harding and Mr Osborn, [and their] happy knack of putting the audience at their ease was primarily responsible for the delightfully informal atmosphere which prevailed throughout the evening."

During the years that followed that "happy knack" evening, Leonard developed a particularly strong bond with the Liverpool Society, a bond that

%o D'Oyly Carte Opera Co,
King's Theatre
Edinburgh.
3·11·47.

Dear Mr. Carte,

I have had a letter from the Head Master of my old school asking me if I can possibly sing on the evening of Wednesday, 12th November when the school will be celebrating its twenty-first birthday.

As we are playing MIKADO, in which I do not appear, that evening, I should be grateful if you would give me permission to travel to London to sing for them.

Yours Sincerely

Leonard Osborn.

A sample of Leonard's handwriting
(D'Oyly Carte Opera Company Archive)

was underscored when he was first elected one of its vice-presidents and then, in 1954, its president; and during these years as a whole he managed occasionally to get to its meetings.

Normally on these occasions his attendance had no outside repercussion. But there was one meeting in March 1953 which – unwittingly - did, the repercussion in question taking the form of a reprimand from the D'Oyly Carte office. It was Frederic Lloyd who had the job of administering the reprimand thought to be required:

> "Dear Mr Osborn (*wrote Lloyd*)
>
> Miss D'Oyly Carte has asked me to write to you as a result of a cutting from the *Liverpool Daily Post* of Wednesday 11th March, in which you are quoted as having informed the members of the Liverpool branch of the Gilbert and Sullivan Society that *The Sorcerer* was to be recorded this summer, and also that there is a possibility of the Company going to America.
>
> Whilst I appreciate that one sometimes finds oneself in a difficult situation of this kind, Miss D'Oyly Carte has asked me to say that she feels it was a little injudicious to make the statement regarding *The Sorcerer*, as this has not yet been announced to the public in any way.
>
> I know that you will appreciate the position."

Quite so!

The Sorcerer recording was to be the first D'Oyly Carte recording since the mass exodus of Company members two years before, and the casting of the various parts on it reflected the changes in the Company personnel and the rise to prominence of new performers since the Martyn Green recordings had been made. Peter Pratt and Ann Drummond-Grant, for instance, sang the patter and contralto roles of John Wellington Wells and Lady Sangazure, while the opera's tenor role of the aristocratic, toffee-nosed Alexis went not to Leonard but to Neville Griffiths.

This may have been at the record company's request rather than being the preferred casting of Bridget and the D'Oyly Carte management. On the other hand, possibly it was. And while Griffiths didn't make any obvious attempt to sound toffee-nosed in the part, he compensated for this by bringing to Alexis's music the strength and fullness of tone that he brought to the singing of the parts he played in the theatre.

The recording of *The Sorcerer* was one of two important D'Oyly Carte events that took place in the summer of 1953. The other was a six week season at Sadler's Wells.

"Oh, Kiss Me, Kiss Me", 1953-57

This latest Sadler's Wells season, which would be the culmination of the 1952-53 tour, was the Company's first Central London season since that at the Savoy two years earlier. It had made sense not to expose the many new and inexperienced performers in the ranks to Central London before they were ready for it, and presumably this was why there had been no such season in 1952.

But they were ready for it now, and it was seen as a season of celebration. For just as the Savoy season had tied up with the Festival of Britain, so this new season tied up with the coronation of the new Queen. Elizabeth II was crowned on June 2nd. D'Oyly Carte opened at Sadler's Wells on the 22nd.

Yet for all that, the Wells season became best known in D'Oyly Carte annals as the season which saw the retirement of Darrell Fancourt; and sadly, unlike the Coronation itself for which everything had gone according to plan, this aspect of things didn't work out the same way. Fancourt was now sixty-five. He had been ill on and off for some time, and towards the end of the Wells season he became ill again.

On the last night, August 1st, he was due to play his most famous part, the Mikado, for the last time. But it was a performance he was dreading, and in the event, perhaps mercifully, he was too ill to go on; so ill, indeed, that just four weeks later he was dead. His final appearance, as it turned out, had been the previous Monday when he'd played Sergeant Meryll in the season's last performance of *The Yeomen of the Guard*.

For Leonard, who had been in his customary role of Fairfax that night, the season had mostly proceeded in a normal way; and the most memorable thing that happened to him during its course were a couple of outbreaks of what might be called encore-itis.

The question of encores in D'Oyly Carte productions – how many should be granted at any given performance and for which particular numbers – was something that caused endless differences of opinion among audiences and fans all through the Company's history. On the one hand there were certain numbers for which an encore was routinely given even when nobody specially wanted it. Then there were other numbers for which, going by the usual audience reaction, an encore would have been more than justified, but which – in post-war performances at any rate – never got one because it had been decided that was the way it was to be.

But there were also those show-stopping numbers (roughly speaking, one per opera) which traditionally received not just one encore but two or more; and there were times when, however many encores these numbers were granted, there were people in the audience who wanted yet another. And this was how, on those two occasions at Sadler's Wells, Leonard got dragged in.

The first of these occasions was a Saturday evening performance of *Yeomen*. The *Yeomen* show-stopper was always the "Cock and Bull" duet between Jack Point and Wilfred Shadbolt part way through Act Two, and at most performances it was encored twice. After the second encore Point and Shadbolt would both go off, and on would come Fairfax who starts his scene with a few lines of dialogue.

Which is what Leonard tried to do on this occasion. But it was one of those occasions when the clamour for another encore hadn't yet subsided, showed indeed no sign of subsiding, and ultimately left him no choice but to abandon his dialogue and go back off stage so as to allow Point and Shadbolt to return and go through their routine once more. Nor was that quite the end of it, for when he duly returned on his own account he was immediately greeted by someone shouting "Your turn now!"

Then a week later there was another, similar occurrence, with Leonard this time one of the participants in the encored number itself. The opera that night was *Iolanthe*, and the encored number was the Act Two dancing trio "If you go in". As with "Cock and Bull" this usually received two encores. Usually, too, there was a clamour for a third; and on this occasion the clamour was so insistent that the early part of the Strephon-Phyllis dialogue that follows the trio was all but completely drowned out – the only difference from the *Yeomen* occasion being that this time the clamourers didn't get their way, and Strephon and Phyllis carried on with their scene regardless.

It was all, so Graham Davis in the *Gilbert & Sullivan Journal* informed his readers, thoroughly bad behaviour; and the only factor he could find in even partial mitigation was that, on the *Yeomen* night, the trouble had been caused not by "any of the regular opera audience" but by people who had spent the day at the Eton-Harrow cricket match at Lord's. And, he added, when it came to the *Iolanthe* night, "nobody was more disgusted than the three artists whose recall was being demanded" – namely Peter Pratt as the Lord Chancellor, Ivor Evans, the evening's Lord Mountararat, and Leonard himself as Tolloller.

But whether this really made Leonard "Disgusted of Sadler's Wells" is another matter. At all events it was unlikely to have affected him or given him pause for as much thought as another happening during the season must have done. That other happening was encapsulated in a brief letter written to him on July 14th by Bridget D'Oyly Carte:

"Dear Mr Osborn

Following our recent conversation, I have decided to ask Mr Griffiths to play the part of Marco in *The Gondoliers*, and this will give you a little more opportunity to rest."

What either of them said in that conversation can, unfortunately, only be guessed at, and it may be that Leonard offered to give up the part without being asked. But even if he'd tried to argue in favour of keeping it, Bridget had a reasonable case for depriving him of it, and was simply resurrecting his supposed need of "more opportunity to rest" as a convenient excuse.

For her real reason for depriving him of the part was one which, understandably, nobody involved was keen to publicise, namely that he'd been increasingly finding the part a vocal strain, with his voice cracking from time to time; and that this was particularly happening when he sang "Take a Pair of sparkling Eyes", the number in which the deficiencies of *any* singer are likely to be noticed most. As Cynthia Morey has written:

"There is simply no way anyone can fake that top B flat, and I would imagine it was becoming out of Leonard's range."

And it wasn't, apparently, only a question of specific notes:

"[Leonard Osborn], who was Marco, gondolier and part king, could have brought a much stricter sense of rhythm to his singing of ... 'Sparkling Eyes'."

(*Harrogate Herald*, January 1952)

Depriving him of Marco, moreover, had the equally justifiable effect of levelling up the available tenor parts between Neville Griffiths and himself. Now each had four parts in the eight full-length operas then in the repertoire. Yet if it was a levelling up in this sense, in another sense it created an imbalance, an imbalance similar to that created by the way the tenor parts had been divided between Leonard and Thomas Round back in 1946-47. Griffiths had already played Marco at occasional performances, so he was not taking on a part that was totally new to him. But playing it on a regular basis meant he would now be appearing in every performance of both *The Gondoliers* and *The Mikado*, which meant by extension that he would be playing in a disproportionate number of shows. And the only consolation for Leonard may have been that those shows would include a disproportionate number of matinees.

This was the way things stood throughout the next (1953-54) tour. But then, for the tour after that (1954-55) another couple of tenor parts entered the reckoning; and the reason for this was the return to the repertoire, for the first time since the war, of *Princess Ida*.

The revival of *Princess Ida* was considered by many people to be the highlight of the entire decade; and on its first night, to quote the *Daily*

Telegraph, there was "a real sizzle of excitement in the air". The date was September 27th 1954. It was the Company's next Central London season; the venue was the Savoy; and of the revived opera's success that night there could be no doubt. The audience, "delighted by everything", as the *Manchester Guardian* critic put it, was roaring for encores before the songs were over and yelling with laughter at the jokes before they were made. "Even if [the production] had been poor – and in fact it was good, with the Company on its toes and full of sparkle – [they] would still have loved every note of it."

When it came to the individual performers, four of them had the parts which, given their respective positions in the Company, naturally fell to them. Just as on *The Sorcerer* recording Peter Pratt had been the natural choice for John Wellington Wells, so now, in *Princess Ida*, he naturally played King Gama. Equally naturally, Ann Drummond-Grant played Lady Blanche; Fisher Morgan played King Hildebrand; and Donald Adams, the successor to Darrell Fancourt, played Arac.

But among the others there were castings that could reasonably be called unexpected. Jeffrey Skitch, for a year now a principal in his own right, despite the fact that Alan Styler was still in the Company, was chosen for Florian; while Joyce Wright, though still very much the principal soubrette, was passed over in favour of Beryl Dixon when it came to Melissa.

Then there were the sopranos and the tenors. There are two principal soprano parts in *Princess Ida*, and the Company had two principal sopranos available to play them – the two being Muriel Harding and the memorably named Tatiana Preston, who had replaced Shirley Hall. The Company management, however, had made another unexpected choice by bringing in a guest artist, Victoria Sladen, to play Ida herself, while shunting Muriel Harding into the secondary part of Lady Psyche and leaving out Tatiana Preston altogether.

With the tenors a similar unexpected casting was made. There are also, as already mentioned, two principal tenor parts in *Ida* – Hilarion the hero and Cyril who, with Florian, make up the trio of dashing young men who scale the wall of Castle Adamant, the Princess's sanctum, in the second act – and the Company had its two resident principal tenors in Leonard and Neville Griffiths. But for Hilarion the management decided to bring in another guest artist. In this case, though, the guest artist was not a newcomer but the instantly recognisable figure of Thomas Round. For Cyril they plumped for Leonard, which meant that Neville Griffiths, like Tatiana Preston, found himself surplus to the opera's requirements.

Having particularly studied the part of Hilarion during his pre-war days in the Company – assuming this is true – Leonard might have envisaged playing Hilarion now. But, for him, Cyril was surely the better option. Cyril is an unashamedly high-spirited, ebullient character, a courtier full of spark and devilment, and with more than a little about him of Dick Dauntless. Where Dauntless has his hornpipe, Cyril has his tipsy "Kissing Song" – a song that positively demanded to be encored, just as the hornpipe demanded to be encored; and as a result, Leonard made almost as much of Cyril as he did of his *Ruddigore* part.

76

Leonard as Cyril with Fisher Morgan as King Hildebrand
(Photograph: Houston Rogers)

The sixteen performances of *Ida* at the Savoy turned out, as it happened, to be the only occasions on which Leonard and Thomas Round worked closely together in the same opera, and the result could hardly have been more gratifying. The part of Hilarion – a splendidly lively part in the middle, but otherwise a more high-flown and essentially romantic part – suited Round as much as Cyril suited Leonard; and it's questionable whether there was ever a trio who worked better together in those parts than the two of *them* and Jeffrey Skitch.

Leonard, though, suffered a minor embarrassment at one of the performances when, according to one D'Oyly Carte habitué, he

> "got totally tangled up in his actions for 'Haughty, humble, coy or free' in the trio 'I am a Maiden', and this didn't go unnoticed. From the audience came calls of 'Fine him! Fine him!' and 'Half a crown!', which finished him off. The trio went on, but he did not contribute much to it after that."

He was also the cause of an unfortunate mishap suffered by Trevor Hills:

> "In *Princess Ida*" (*Hills relates*) "I played Scynthius, one of King Gama's three sons, and in the fight scene in Act Three we each had to duel with Hilarion, Florian and Cyril in turn. In one performance, to make sure I went down at the end, Cyril (Osborn) gave me a hard push, and I landed on my tail-bone, which got cracked. Later, after I left the Carte, I had to have an operation to cure the damage. So I have a painful memory of Osborn."

Very different, and much more cheerful, is an anecdote relating to the effect Leonard's playing of the part had on the opposite sex. It's an anecdote that comes from another D'Oyly Carte habitué, Michael Walters:

> "I remember many years ago asking a then prominent member of the London Gilbert and Sullivan Society what it was about Osborn [that made him so special] and she replied: 'When, as Cyril, he sang 'Oh, kiss me, kiss me' he had no need to say it more than once!'
> I think that sums it up."

Leonard's pleas to be kissed, moreover, were not only heard by people in the theatre. On *Princess Ida's* first night, the second act was broadcast on the radio by the BBC. *Ida*, indeed, was one of three of the operas broadcast in whole or part during or shortly after the Savoy season. The second was *Ruddigore* and the third (broadcast on Boxing Day) was *The Mikado*. A tape of that *Mikado* broadcast still survives, and copies are now even available on CD. Sadly the equivalent tapes of the *Ida* and *Ruddigore* broadcasts have long since disappeared – though having said that, it's worth adding that a very considerable amount of material of this sort has come to light in recent years, and the chance of them turning up sometime can't be totally discounted.

Leonard, of course, doesn't feature in *The Mikado* broadcast. But he did feature in a broadcast of *Iolanthe* a year earlier. And still on the subject of broadcasts, it's also worth noting that back in 1952 plans had been made to televise *Cox and Box*, with Leonard playing Box, and a couple of dates were actually fixed for its transmission. But that was as far as it got. That was one broadcast that never took place.

Back, though, to *Princess Ida*, for as well as the broadcast the Company made an LP recording of the opera which was issued by Decca in 1955. This turned out to be the last recording Leonard was to make; and speaking for the many people who feel it's definitely one of his best ones, here is another G&S enthusiast, Marcia Menter:

"Though I never saw him perform, he's a sentimental favourite of mine, and I like his recordings very much even when his voice is threadbare, which it often is. His Cyril is completely irresistible, and I'll bet he himself was pretty irresistible, at least as a performer."

The *Ida* recording, moreover, is a particularly valuable record of the production itself, in that its cast was without exception the cast that had played it on stage. On stage, that is, at the Savoy; for the two guest artists had been engaged purely for the Savoy season. Once that season was over – it finished on December 11th – both had to be replaced in their parts; and both, getting back to normal, were replaced from within the Company itself. Victoria Sladen gave way to Muriel Harding, thereby elevating the latter from Lady Psyche to Ida herself – to sighs of relief all round, as it was universally agreed that Sladen had not been a success. By contrast Thomas Round, as previously implied, had done splendidly, and his place as Hilarion was not so easy to fill.

It could – maybe even should – have been filled by Neville Griffiths. Alternatively Leonard could have been switched to Hilarion from Cyril, with Griffiths taking over the latter part. Privately, in a letter to a friend, Graham Davis voiced the opinion that it was "not outside the bounds of imagination to think of Griffiths as Cyril". Yet the decision actually made was, to say the least, surprising: the management passed over Griffiths for both parts and, while keeping Leonard as Cyril, gave Hilarion to a tenor chorister, John Fryatt.

From a review of the opera in Birmingham the following May:

"Among other strong points [there was] a most agreeable young tenor in John Fryatt … The fooling of the two male trios is generally excellent, but Leonard Osborn grievously overdoes it in his Kissing Song"

- a rare instance where Leonard's acting, rather than his singing, came in for any sort of criticism.

But what, in the weeks and months that followed *Ida's* long-awaited return to the D'Oyly Carte repertoire … what of the production as a whole? While there was no question regarding the success it achieved at the Savoy, it failed to make quite the same impact when performed on tour, and was not (as

John Fryatt (top) as Hilarion and Jeffrey Skitch (below) as Florian
(Photographs: Houston Rogers and G&S Photos)

Ruddigore had been on its revival six years earlier) the box office draw the management had hoped it would be. Nor were its fortunes helped by the fact that it couldn't be played in the smaller theatres the Company visited because its scenery was too large to fit into them.

But against that it was taken as part of the repertoire on the Company's next American visit.

That visit, the fourth American visit in which Leonard took part, was the most ambitious of those visits by some distance. It was publicised as marking the seventy-fifth anniversary of the first D'Oyly Carte American visit in 1879-80. It lasted no fewer than eight months (June 1955-February 1956). And it took in eleven venues, nine in America and two in Canada.

There were, though, a few days when the plans made for it looked like having to be modified before it even got under way. It had been arranged that, as in 1947, the Company would sail on the *Queen Mary*. But a strike by the ship's staff kept the *Queen Mary* immobile in Southampton, and it took a flurry of activity behind the scenes before it was arranged that, for the first time ever, they would fly to America instead. For many – probably most – of those involved, flying was a whole new experience; and, despite his years in the RAF, it may even have been a new experience for Leonard.

And certainly flying solved the immediate problem; that is, getting the Company where they needed to be – so much so that, from the moment they took off, everything went swimmingly, and the whole visit proved a seemingly unending triumph.

"This is the first Martyn Green-less engagement of the Company for a good many years," wrote a reviewer when, following seasons in Central City in Colorado, San Francisco, Los Angeles and Chicago, they arrived for an eight and a half week run in New York. (Entering America through the back door didn't seem to matter this time.) And that reviewer had latched on to a salient point, for Martyn Green was, if anything, an even bigger name in America than he'd been at home.

His absence, indeed, could have left both critics and audiences with a sense of dissatisfaction, a feeling that the current personnel were not going to be as good as those who had made the American trip on previous occasions. But any concern of that nature was quickly overcome wherever they went, and that included New York itself. The Company "is giving us the finest Gilbert and Sullivan we have had for years," claimed the reviewer quoted above, after they'd given just one performance in the city, and at no time did he or any other reviewer find cause to seriously modify that judgment.

As for the individuals who made up the current Company, Peter Pratt naturally attracted the most attention and gained the most effusive notices, as he generally did at home. Here are just two from the *San Francisco Chronicle*:

"Peter Pratt, the Lord Chancellor, is probably the only man alive who can remind you of Charlie Chaplin, Danny Kaye and Woodrow Wilson in a single paragraph, and still leave plenty of margin for his own characterisation."

"The melancholy jester, the clown with a broken heart, is of all theatrical characters the one most difficult to realise without coarseness or bathos. Peter Pratt [as Jack Point] walked that tightrope with consummate agility and grace."

But naturally, too, praise (in San Francisco or anywhere else) wasn't bestowed on him alone. For instance:

"Ann Drummond-Grant, singing over a rush of San Francisco fog to the throat, was still a memorable Buttercup."
"Fisher Morgan as Pooh-Bah looked and sounded exactly like Sir Winston Churchill."
"Donald Adams, who rejoices in one of the most colossal bass voices ever to adorn a Gilbert and Sullivan cast, played the Mikado in the flinty cruel and overwhelming style of the Savoyard tradition."
"Alan Styler plays and sings Strephon with an almost Mozartian elegance." (Gosh!)

And if Neville Griffiths was described as "unfortunately on the mediocre side" as Nanki-Poo, he came good in the reviewer's eyes in *HMS Pinafore*:

"Neville Griffiths found his vocal sea legs as Ralph Rackstraw, and proved that a Gilbert and Sullivan tenor can be an excellent musician and even, at times, a subtle one."

While as for Leonard:

"One will go many a day before witnessing a more gallant hero than Leonard Osborn [as Colonel Fairfax]"

And

"Leonard Osborn's Lord Tolloller has several virtues; the least but most extraordinary of them is that it provides us with the experience of hearing an English actor parody an upper-crust English accent."

And if, taking the American visit as a whole, his name once again cropped up less than it might have done, the reason this time was the arrangement of the repertoire. He did all right in New York where the programme included both *Princess Ida* and *Ruddigore* and where, in addition to Fairfax and Tolloller, he accordingly played Cyril and Dick Dauntless. But *Patience* wasn't brought on this visit at all, while away from New York the only operas played throughout were *The Mikado*, *HMS Pinafore*, *Trial by Jury* and *Iolanthe*. And given that, of these, he only appeared in *Iolanthe*, this meant that in certain towns he was not involved in well over half the performances.

No D'Oyly Carte tour – and certainly no D'Oyly Carte tour of America – ever consisted of performances (and rehearsals) alone. In town after town there was in addition a whole raft of receptions, parties, lunches and private hospitality given and offered in their honour. There was the excitement of sightseeing. There was the excitement – and exhaustion – of long train journeys between one town and the next.

And on this 1955-56 tour there was excitement in the fact that three Company marriages took place. Jeffrey Skitch married a girl he met in Los Angeles. Herbert Newby, now Assistant Stage Manager, married Ceinwen Jones, one of the choristers. While Jon Ellison married Joy Mornay, another chorister, and has a vivid memory of Leonard which he associates with this:

> "A day or two after the wedding I had an accident with a bowl of hot tomato soup, which splashed up on to my face, giving me a really bad scald. A huge blister formed on one cheek, which the doctor I consulted burst to drain it of fluid.
>
> As a result I had to miss a show, *HMS Pinafore*, though this gave me the opportunity to watch my one and only show, ever, from the front of house. I did return the following day, but had to make up my good cheek to match the burnt one!
>
> One evening during this period Leonard came to our hotel room to commiserate with me. He was really nice and comforting. He also brought us a little gift of a coffee percolator, and said we should use it throughout the tour.
>
> We still have that percolator, and it is a very treasured piece of our memorabilia. Whenever it catches my eye, I always think very kindly of Leonard."

Among the receptions, lunches and other events that made up the social side of the tour there was one splendid oddity: a cricket match – a "long awaited challenge match" - between a D'Oyly Carte team and the crew of *HMS Superb* somewhere near Los Angeles. Leonard was almost certainly involved in this, if not as a player then as an umpire, a role he took on for D'Oyly Carte cricket matches back in Britain.

In addition he almost certainly played some golf on the tour, and having at one time been treasurer ("that honorary, honourable and official capacity," as he described it) of the Company's Golf Circle, he was now – an even greater honour – its captain. Its president, it is worth noting, was Bridget D'Oyly Carte herself, and among the letters from Leonard to be found in the D'Oyly Carte Archive there is one dated April 16th 1954 thanking her for her "very generous subscription".

The American visit reached its conclusion with a ten day season in Philadelphia beginning on January 30th 1956. Then it was time at last for the Company to return to England. This time there was no strike to cause them to alter their travelling arrangements, and they returned as planned by sea. On February 22nd they docked at Southampton, and just five days later they resumed their normal touring at home with a two week season in Bournemouth, followed by a three week season in Golders Green. Golders Green Hippodrome was my own local theatre.

Since that exhilarating *Ruddigore* at Sadler's Wells almost seven years before, I had been to D'Oyly Carte performances just three times: *The Yeomen of the Guard* and *The Mikado* at Golders Green in 1950 and *Princess Ida* at the Savoy in 1954. This meant that, though my D'Oyly Carte-going stretched back to 1945, I had yet to see the Company in *Iolanthe*, *The Gondoliers*, *The Pirates of Penzance* and *Trial by Jury*. It also meant, though I didn't know it at the time, that I would never see Leonard as Marco, Frederic or the Defendant. But at Golders Green in 1956 I was going for the first time to see *Iolanthe*, and thus for the first time to see him as Tolloller.

Iolanthe was being performed on the first Tuesday of the season, and that evening I went with my father. Dad, as I mentioned at the beginning of this book, had been immensely impressed by Leonard as Dick Dauntless, and he was now impressed by his Tolloller – as I was myself. He was also particularly impressed by Peter Pratt (once again the Lord Chancellor), Donald Adams (Mountararat) and Cynthia Morey (Phyllis), and so was I by the three of them too. But that's three other stories, if not more, and I'm afraid they'll have to wait – at least for the time being.

Two nights after *Iolanthe* I saw my first *Trial* and *Pirates*. *Pirates* I loved, but *Trial* I found disappointing, and I continued to find it disappointing in the years that followed – a D'Oyly Carte production that never quite seemed to get off the ground. There were, I eventually came to realise, two or three reasons for this, and one of those reasons was the casting. *Trial by Jury* needs a strong cast, but because it was never more than an adjunct to the main programme, it didn't always get one.

That was certainly true as regards the Defendant. The Defendant who (as indeed is the case with all the other characters) is never alone on stage, needs to be a performer of vibrant personality who can stand out from the crowd rather than, as happened too often, be submerged by it. He needs to be someone you instinctively watch, someone with the instant attractiveness of a shameless Lothario who has members of the opposite sex falling for him at the twist of his little finger. And while I always regretted never having seen Leonard as Marco or Frederic, I always regretted still more that I never saw him relishing the attentions of the *Trial by Jury* bridesmaids as the Defendant.

As that Golders Green season progressed I also saw Leonard for the second time as Dick Dauntless, Fairfax and Cyril – though not the Duke of Dunstable, since *Patience* was still out of the repertoire and continued to remain so for months afterwards. It eventually made its return in a new production during the Company's next Central London season (December 1956-March 1957), the venue for which was the Princes Theatre in Shaftesbury Avenue. As with the Sadler's Wells season seven years earlier, this season opened with *Ruddigore* ("Leonard Osborn was a spick-and-span Richard Dauntless" – the *Daily Telegraph*) and during the course of its thirteen weeks I saw him for the third time as Dauntless and Fairfax (though not as Cyril – it had now become the turn of *Princess Ida* to be dropped from the repertoire) and the second time as the Duke and Tolloller.

Then at Oxford in May I saw him as Tolloller twice more (twice in a *day*, as it happened – that's what comes of growing up) and at Streatham Hill in

Donald Adams (top) as Lord Mountararat and Leonard (below) as Tolloller
(Photographs: G&S Photos)

December was to see him as Tolloller again. If as Dauntless he was out on his own, and his Cyril made a strong runner up, his Tolloller was, for me, never that far behind.

This chapter might have ended there. But it doesn't for two reasons – two reasons which, between them, had to do with the three most significant women in his life. The first of them relates to his mother, Louisa.

Louisa Osborn, for many years now a widow, had for a considerable period been helping to run a transport café in central Croydon. The café, a flourishing business, was owned by her other son – which is to say, Leonard's elder brother Frederick. Frederick Osborn is described by one person who came across him during this period as "a typical South London gorblimey character, totally different from Leonard". He was an experienced cook, having been a cook prior to going into the Army (which in typical Army fashion ignored his culinary skills and made him instead a wireless operator in the Tank Corps). And in the café he ran the back area and did the cooking here too, while his mother served the customers out front.

The most interesting fact about her time in the café, though, is that she festooned the walls with photographs of Leonard in his various G&S roles. Was she, even if she never said it in so many words, proud of his achievements? As though to suggest this may well have been the case, there is a letter in the D'Oyly Carte Archive which she wrote to the London office during the American tour of 1955, asking for "a list of the theatres [sic] the D'Oyly Carte Opera Company are visiting during the weeks … in New York". Presumably Leonard had never got round to telling her this himself.

The second reason for going on with this chapter has even more significance: nothing less than the reappearance in his life of Margaret Mitchell. The letter he had received from her at Stratford back in 1953 had not proved the end of their relationship after all. Well within a year it was on again, and she was turning up from time to time at this or that theatre where the Company were playing, specially to see him. And Leonard was quite patently overjoyed. Jon Ellison, who hadn't come across her or seen the two of them together before, remembers him being "all bouncy and rather like a schoolboy whilst she was around – quite unlike the normal Leonard, in fact."

She also turned up, along with other past D'Oyly Carte figures, at the Savoy Hotel at a party given to wish the Company well before they set off for the American tour. She stood there in tears, Jon Ellison says, as they drew away; and was actually in New York with a Scottish singing group at some point when D'Oyly Carte were ensconced *there*.

Then, out of the blue, came more or less a repeat of what had happened before. Leonard and Eileen, his wife, had been going through divorce proceedings. The exact chronology is unclear, but either when the divorce had actually come through or when it was close to doing so, Leonard asked Margaret to marry him. And her response, however seductively delivered, was blunt: "Leonard, darling, I'll continue having an affair with you, but I don't want to marry you."

His emotional world was shattered once more. He had, it seems clear, pinned his hopes for years on the two of them eventually getting married. And what she'd now said – and the way she'd said it – turned that hope to dust; led, indeed, to them breaking up a second time. And this time the break-up was final. But it would surely have been hard for anyone to guess or foretell the sequel.

For the sequel was this: the third woman in his life now came back into the picture. He got together with Eileen again.

They were brought together sometime during the first half of 1957 by a man named Arthur Richards. Richards was then the D'Oyly Carte heavy baritone, having replaced Fisher Morgan in this capacity the year before. To many people's surprise, says Jeffrey Skitch, he and Leonard seemed to hit it off together, and when it came to helping people with personal problems Richards obviously had what it took. On June 27th 1957, little more than three months after their divorce had been made absolute, Eileen and Leonard re-married.

Telegrams came from Frederic Lloyd and another stalwart of the D'Oyly Carte office, the Company's Assistant Secretary, Albert Truelove. "Very best wishes for today and for your future happiness"; that was the one from Lloyd. "Every happiness to you both"; that was the one from Truelove.

Perhaps, this time round, "true love" would be the lasting outcome.

Leonard at a stage door

"Careful Handling", 1957-58

By contrast with what had happened in his private and emotional life, the four years covered by the previous chapter were, professionally, the most secure and settled of all Leonard's years in D'Oyly Carte, at least since his return to the Company in 1946. During those years – effectively the autumn of 1953 to that of 1957 - he'd had no further trouble with his voice. There were no brushes with the management, or at any rate none for which any evidence has come to light. He was unchallenged in his five parts, the five parts in the full-length operas that without question suited him best.

But unfortunately that sense of security was not to last much longer. As 1957 drew towards its close, problems with his performances began to gnaw at him once more. And as at the times they'd gnawed at him before, those problems centred round his singing voice and its propensity to crack in its upper register. This was always most likely to occur, he actually and without prompting told Tony Gower, in low-lying places near water such as Stratford-upon-Avon where the theatre is right by the river, and where the Company played a four week season over the Christmas-New Year period of 1957-58.

For the first months of 1958, admittedly, things were somewhat up and down, with times when the problem seemed acute interspersed with other times when it seemed to go away altogether. But the mere fact of its resurgence meant that sooner or later the difficulties it was causing him were bound to come to a head, and they did so in the second half of the summer. On July 22nd Frederic Lloyd sent the following memo to Bridget D'Oyly Carte:

"Mr Osborn accepts salary of forty pounds for tour starting 8th September 1958" [Bridget had refused him a rise back in 1953, but had raised him to forty pounds a week after the 1955-56 American tour] "but in the event of his voice failing, if Miss Carte wishes him to leave, he would not raise any objection, and a satisfactory solution can be arrived at.

I saw Mr Osborn and had a long talk to him about his voice. He also is very conscious of the fact that he is not singing up to standard.

However he told me that he thought it was partly due to an attack of Asian flu which he had last autumn, which has left him with bad catarrh. I told him that I did not think it could be, as the criticisms had been levelled at him long before Asian flu was ever heard of.

He wondered whether it was lack of work, for sometimes he has periods when he is not singing at all; however I told him he could always practise. He told me that when he is in the dressing room he can always sing well, but as soon as he gets on the stage he is gripped by a terrible attack of nerves and he feels he needs confidence.

He has not been to a singing teacher [for some time] and I have strongly recommended to him that he should find one, and have suggested one or two people.

Mr Osborn certainly sang better in *Ruddigore* than I have heard him for some time."

There are two points in particular to highlight in this memo. First, its date: July 22nd 1958. And second, the statement that Leonard was prepared at any time to leave D'Oyly Carte without quibbling if asked to do so. The significance of these two points will become apparent in due course.

What the memo makes clear, though, is that his future in the Company was now in a state of uncertainty; and the new (1958-59) tour was little more than a month old when the next development occurred. This took the form of a "private and confidential" letter from Lloyd to Leonard himself. The letter was dated October 13th, and the "forthcoming London season" to which he referred was due to begin in mid-December:

"Dear Mr Osborn

I am writing to you personally because several complaints have been made, and also press notices have not been too good regarding your recent performances, particularly in *Yeomen*. Miss D'Oyly Carte is, not unnaturally, somewhat concerned regarding the forthcoming London season.

As you may remember, we have had several discussions over the past months about this matter and, when I last saw you in Coventry, I think you told me you were beginning lessons with an Italian teacher.

The point that really arises is – is he doing you any good, and is there anything further that can be done to overcome the difficulties? I know it may not be easy for you to get down to London while you are on tour, but from the time we finish in Liverpool until you yourself start with the Opera Company in London – and this is for your private information – you will have about four weeks without performances. This will give you some time to study with your new teacher, and I do most sincerely hope, in all seriousness, he will be able to help you overcome the trouble.

It may be, of course, that you have not been well lately, or there is some perfectly simple explanation for this trouble, and, if so, if there is any help I can give you I should be only too pleased to do so."

Five days later (October 18th) Leonard replied:

"Dear Mr Lloyd

Your letter, with its charges of 'several complaints' and 'press notices not too good', came as a great shock and with a shattering of confidence. I have read and re-read it many times – a form of masochism, I guess.

The teacher with whom I had a few lessons – Rodolfo Mele – was helping me in my difficulty. Difficulty! Let's face it, I crack on a note that I can normally sing standing on my head! I had already decided to go to him again during the London season. The only thing is, he is expensive: at two and [a] half guineas a lesson I cannot afford more than one lesson a week, though I would prefer to go to him at least twice a week.

During the few times I was with him I was singing my solos and other more difficult ones with great ease, and no suggestion of cracking – but, let it be noted, in an atmosphere which engendered confidence and a dispelling of tension.

As I say, I shall be going to him when we get to London, and I am sure he will help me, and that there will be no more cause for complaints. Perhaps you would ring him. I haven't got his phone number, but he is the only MELE in the book. I know he will put things right for me."

Lloyd meanwhile was keeping Bridget up to date with the situation, as it was his responsibility to do. The day before Leonard wrote that letter, he (Lloyd) reported a conversation his secretary Joan Robertson had had with C. William (Billy) Morgan, for many years a D'Oyly Carte chorister and understudy and, briefly, Assistant Stage Manager, and by now a sort of unofficial elder statesman. Morgan had had a meeting with Leonard a month before, and had found him "still very emotionally upset over the events of last year leading to his re-marriage"; while on the question of Leonard having more singing lessons, Morgan told Joan Robertson he felt these were pointless. Leonard, in his opinion, was now too old for lessons to be any use. "I think that with careful handling," wrote Lloyd to Bridget, "we shall be able to get Mr Osborn through the London season, but we must probably make up our minds that this will be his last tour."

Three days later he notified her of the arrival of Leonard's letter, which he described as "slightly unpleasant", and said that he was completely unconvinced by Leonard's claim that he couldn't afford more than one singing lesson a week on a salary of forty pounds. Nonetheless he was careful not to mention this to Leonard himself when, on October 23rd, he wrote to him again:

"Dear Mr Osborn

Thank you for your letter of the 18th October.

I am a little surprised at the attitude you have taken, as my letter was in no way intended to be hurtful to you – in fact, very much to the contrary. I read and heard with disappointment the criticisms, and wrote to you as I felt it was my duty to find out from you personally how you were progressing with your new teacher.

I fully appreciate it is difficult for you to come down and see him in London when you are in Scotland" [the Company were then playing a three week season in Glasgow, and were about to follow it with a season of the same length in Edinburgh] "but I am extremely glad to hear that he has given you confidence and is dispelling tension. I am sure that the period you will be with him at the beginning of the London season will be invaluable to you."

This correspondence is revealing, and in certain respects surprisingly so. The D'Oyly Cartes had a reputation, admittedly at times deserved, for treating their performers insensitively, harshly, even callously or whatever word of similar import you care to use. But insensitivity, harshness or callousness are not words that can reasonably be used to describe Bridget's and Frederic Lloyd's treatment of Leonard here.

That Leonard had problems was admitted by Leonard himself. Given this, and in the face of complaints about his performances (from whoever those complaints emanated) and poor press notices, they had to enquire what he was doing about his problems and find out – to put it bluntly – if he was still up to the job. Had they not done so they would have risked portraying themselves as indifferent to the Company's standards, as well as appearing to display something like contempt for their audiences.

Moreover, far from taking an insensitive approach, Lloyd was demonstrating a clear concern for Leonard's welfare. If Bridget and he were looking for an excuse to ask Leonard to leave the Company, they surely had one now – and equally surely they allowed the opportunity to pass. They issued no warnings, no threats. Rather than showing a desire to give him the push, they seemed genuinely anxious to get him right again and to keep him on – at any rate for the time being.

It may be, indeed, that they were reluctant to lose a performer who still, as they were aware, had enormous drawing power. A letter to a magazine called *Picturegoer*, probably drafted by Lloyd though signed by Joan Robertson, included the sentence "He is certainly one of the most popular members of the Company and has, I believe, a great female following". Granted that letter was written the year before, in September 1957. But there was nothing to suggest this aspect of things had changed since then, whatever else may have done.

Arguably the most surprising aspect of the correspondence from the London end – and the same applied to all the correspondence on the subject of Leonard's voice that had engaged the management previously – was something that was not mentioned or alluded to even once: the name of Isidore Godfrey and what *he* felt about the problem. Yet surely his views would have been as pertinent to the issue as anybody's. Surely he might at the very least have been asked for suggestions as to how Leonard could be helped or how he could help himself.

What does the correspondence reveal about Leonard himself? The answer here is a state of edginess, a state of defensiveness and self-doubt, a state of worry, even of denial, about what was happening to him. His re-marriage, which might have had a calming effect on him, had demonstrably not had that effect – or had not had it yet. At the back of his mind must have been the thought that he might at any time be asked to leave the Company; and even though he had indicated he was prepared to go, that didn't necessarily mean he *wanted* to go. Down the years many performers had been asked to leave. Only that summer this had happened to Neville Griffiths.

Griffiths left the Company at the end of that year's tour in July, and personally I felt sad to see him go. A comment on his record card implied that his voice was no longer quite what it had been. But even if this *was* the case, it was only part of the reason he was pushed out. The prime reason was that the management now had another slimmer, and altogether more stylish and glamorous tenor to take his place. This glamorous replacement was none other than Thomas Round, returning as a full member of the Company after nine years.

According to the latter's autobiography, Frederic Lloyd had telephoned him earlier that year inviting him to return, and to do so, furthermore, on nothing less than an unheard of (for D'Oyly Carte) five year contract. Since leaving the Company in 1949 he (Round) had had a highly successful career with Sadler's Wells and other managements and had become something of a star, a "box office tenor", in one journalist's phrase, widely known in the light operatic field.

Consequently for D'Oyly Carte he was now a real catch. He took over three of the parts he had played in his first D'Oyly Carte incarnation – Nanki-Poo, Ralph Rackstraw and Frederic – along with Marco, the other part previously played by Griffiths; and the quick and assured way in which he slotted back into the Company could be seen as another factor threatening Leonard's own position.

Yet it's equally possible that Round's return may have worked to Leonard's advantage, may have helped influence Bridget's and Lloyd's decision to hang on to him in spite of his problems, if only to avoid having to absorb two new principal tenors into the Company simultaneously.

And it's also worth making the point that Leonard's notices at this time were not all poor as Lloyd in his letter had appeared to suggest. "Mixed" was a fairer description, as is clear from the following four examples drawn from those three weeks the Company spent in Glasgow:

"Leonard Osborn's Fairfax was dignified and well drawn, but vocally it lacked fluency and his singing was off colour."

(The *Scotsman*)

"And in the role of Richard Dauntless, Leonard Osborn's vocal limitations are more than compensated by his easy acting and his deft dancing, particularly of the sailor's hornpipe."

(The Bulletin)

"Leonard Osborn was in good voice as Dauntless, and danced his hornpipe neatly."

(Glasgow Evening Times)

"Leonard Osborn as Earl Tolloller was the epitome of aristocratic dignity and magnificence."

(The Scotsman)

So while a cause for concern, such notices hardly added up to disaster. Moreover, at the Royal Court Theatre in Liverpool which the Company played in November, there was even a celebration. On Wednesday the 26th, between a matinee and the evening performance of *Patience*, the Company assembled on the stage for a ceremony to mark the twenty-first anniversary of Leonard's first joining D'Oyly Carte.

The centrepiece of this ceremony was a cake made to the design of John Laidman Stell, a keen D'Oyly Carte follower and art master at Chester City Grammar School. It was a design that featured a surround of specially painted little panels, each representing one of the parts Leonard had played, and the whole cake was topped with twenty-one candles and a miniature coronet modelled on the coronet he wore as Lord Tolloller. Leonard, all smiles, cut the cake (or at any rate made the first incision) with the sword he wore as the Duke of Dunstable.

And while it had not been Liverpool that had first seen him on stage in the Company, it was by no means inappropriate that Liverpool should have been the venue for the ceremony, for according to one of the local papers, he had more friends there "than anywhere else except his native London" – a comment reflecting in part his continued association with the city's branch of the G&S Society.

The day after the celebration, in fact, he gave an evening's entertainment to the branch, on this occasion – not for the first time – having Alan Styler with him to help things along. And as well as that, he used the occasion to present the branch with a silver cup, a trophy to be competed for by local groups presenting scenes from the operas. It was as though his period of self-doubt and nervous tension had passed.

And yet … it was either just before or just after these two occasions that he suffered a blackout, a blackout sufficiently bad to induce a temporary loss of memory. True, the blackout was brief. He soon recovered and was back to normal. But nervous tension may well have been its cause.

The Liverpool season closed on November 29th, and the Company had an unusual two week break from performances before their next date, the thirteen week London season to which everything that autumn had been leading up.

Leonard, dressed as the Duke of Dunstable, with his "twenty-first anniversary"
cake
(Melvyn Tarran collection)

"A Thousand Thanks, Good Sir", 1959

Looking back, the 1958-59 London season can be seen as the climax – the triumphant culmination – of the whole decade. The venue, as two years previously, was the Princes Theatre, since the 1920s second only to the Savoy in its emotional connotations for the members of the Company and their audiences. And never since the 1920s had a season been more eagerly awaited. Never had excitement and anticipation been greater.

It opened on December 15th with a week's performances of a new production of *The Gondoliers*. The second week – Christmas week – was given over to *The Mikado*. Then, beginning on December 29th, came week three: a week of *The Yeomen of the Guard*.

Not being in either *The Gondoliers* or *The Mikado*, Leonard that season had yet to appear – the only one of the principals to whom this applied. For him those first two weeks, when added to the previous two week break, made up the four weeks without performances that Frederic Lloyd had referred to as his chance to have a solid block of time with his new singing teacher.

But now, with *Yeomen*, his return to the scene had come at last. And when on the Monday evening the audience assembled, all those people who read their programmes would have duly seen his name against Fairfax's name in the cast list, and would have expected him to make his first entrance on stage at the appropriate moment.

All those people would have expected it except, that is, about ten of them: a group of students and other enthusiasts of similar age sitting in a line up in the gallery. For when the members of that group opened their programmes they found inside them a printed "indulgence slip" informing them that "at this performance the part of Colonel Fairfax will be played by Frederick Sinden" and, by implication, that Leonard wouldn't be appearing that night after all.

Consternation! Then, suddenly, there were bursts of laughter as some of the group twigged. One of their number owned a small printing machine. The indulgence slip was a spoof slipped into their programmes primarily to disconcert one of the girls who regarded Leonard as her special pin-up. And disconcert her it undoubtedly did – though even then some of the group weren't totally reassured till Fairfax eventually made his entrance and they could see it really was Leonard.

I was one of that group, and was fooled as much as any of them. Clustering near the stage door after the performance, we all got Leonard to sign our copies of the spoof. I still have my own copy, kept as a treasured memento – and this is a minor miracle because I nearly lost it straight afterwards. Below the word "Leonard" in "Leonard Meryll" (see below) is a grey mark. That mark was made by the point of an umbrella which pinned it to the platform on Tottenham Court Road Station, and saved it from going down on to the line when it somehow fluttered out of the programme as I waited for my tube home.

If for Leonard's particular fans that *Yeomen* week was the first real high spot of the season, the second high spot immediately succeeded it. The following Monday, January 5th 1959, *Yeomen* was replaced by *Princess Ida*. By this time *Princess Ida* had not been played anywhere for over a year, and there were a couple of major changes in the cast compared with that of the opera's original revival. Ida herself was now being played by Jean Hindmarsh, who had replaced Muriel Harding in 1956. King Hildebrand would be played by Kenneth Sandford, successor to Arthur Richards who had stayed in the Company for just a year.

Surprisingly, though, John Fryatt retained Hilarion – surprisingly because, with Thomas Round's return to the Company, he might have been expected to relinquish it in Round's favour given the success the latter had made of it in 1954; surprising at any rate to the uninformed outsider. Contractual arrangements – who had been asked and signed an agreement to play which parts that year – were probably the reason. But Peter Pratt was still King Gama. Jeffrey Skitch was still Florian. And Leonard was still Cyril.

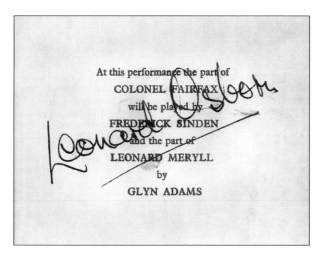

The spoof indulgence slip

Thanks at least partly to the fact it was played so rarely, *Princess Ida* was for many people the prime attraction of the season; and because of this there was considerable disappointment expressed that it was scheduled for just four performances. This was a meagre total, especially when compared with the twenty-six performances scheduled for *The Mikado* and the twenty allotted to *The Gondoliers*. Moreover those four performances were bunched together in that one week – on the Monday; the Tuesday; and the Wednesday when it was played twice.

So all four performances were special – and a number of enthusiasts were present at all four. But at the same time there was no doubt that the Monday performance was even more special than the others, because it marked the seventy-fifth anniversary of *Ida's* first ever performance. *Iolanthe* had been given an equivalent anniversary performance a little over a year before – a "slap-up performance", as the *Daily Telegraph* called it – and *Ida's* anniversary performance now was pretty slap-up too.

Curiously, though I was there, I recall almost no details about the performance as such. But against that I have one overriding memory of the occasion, a memory on a par with the occasion at Sadler's Wells all but ten years earlier when I first saw *Ruddigore*. Though it didn't fully dawn on me till afterwards, I realised I hadn't been able to take my eyes off Leonard that night all the time he was on stage. I ought at that age (nearly twenty-one) to have been eyeing up the young ladies in the chorus. But I wasn't. Leonard simply overshadowed them. If I wanted an example of the pull he exerted over his audiences both male and female, that's the example I'd choose.

Later in the season I saw him as the Duke of Dunstable. Again I remember scarcely any of the details. Yet of one thing I'm fairly certain: that at none of the performances in which I saw him that season was there any sense that his voice might be going to crack. So had his new teacher been successful and really got him sorted out at last? There had been performances in the past when, along with others in the "group", I'd been on edge every time he sang wondering if he was going to be all right. But not that season at the Princes. And he was still in confident vocal form when, on March 14th, it came to the season's Last Night.

The Last Night was another of those D'Oyly Carte "surprise" nights, when what was to be performed was not announced in advance but kept secret from the audience right up to the moment the curtain rose on each act. On this occasion the programme consisted of, first, Act Two of *Iolanthe*, with Leonard as Tolloller. Then, second, came Act Two of *The Gondoliers*, in which he had no part.

These two acts were played virtually straight. But when it came to the third and final act it was a different matter altogether. That third act turned out to be *Trial by Jury*; and with *Trial by Jury* that night, the D'Oyly Carte Company let their hair down in a way that, given their reputation for doing things rigidly by the book, was truly astonishing.

For though all the performers adhered throughout the proceedings to the correct words and music, they were all dressed in totally *in*correct fashion in costumes from all the other operas in the season's repertoire except *Cox and*

Box and *Trial by Jury* itself. John Fryatt as the Defendant, for example, was dressed as Ralph Rackstraw. Jeffrey Skitch as the Counsel was dressed in the academic robes he wore as Florian. And not only that, but all the other principals, who didn't normally appear in *Trial* at all, were there, similarly mis-dressed, as spectators and members of the public, and each of them made his or her own contribution to the collective fun. Kenneth Sandford, dressed as the Sergeant of Police, went round the chorus of bridesmaids with a large box of chocolates. Peter Pratt, dressed as the Duke of Plaza-Toro, raised aloft two banners, one of which read "Trying Tonight".

As for Leonard, he and Donald Adams were solidly ensconced together downstage right, Leonard in his Tolloller robes and Donald Adams dressed as the Pirate King. They spent part of the time reading a copy of *Lady Chatterley's Lover*, then very much the book of the moment; and on the entrance of the Judge and the Usher's command "in due submission bend", they both "dropped to their knees with abject oriental salaams". One could not but admire, wrote Graham Davis, how brilliantly the two of them played up to each other.

Which will have surprised nobody after seeing them earlier in the evening (or at any other time) perform their dialogue scene as Tolloller and Mountararat in the second act of *Iolanthe*.

Once again looking back, that Princes season and the Last Night in particular can be seen not just as the climax of the decade, but as the beginning of the end of another D'Oyly Carte era. Given the preponderance in the G&S scheme of things of the performer who played the "patter parts", that era may be described as the "Peter Pratt Era".

But now, in mid-May, it was announced that Pratt was leaving the Company, and by the beginning of June he was gone in all but name. In mid-September Ann Drummond-Grant, who could more or less be described as his co-star, died at the tragically early age of fifty-four.

Then there was Leonard.

Leonard seemed definitely to have come through his bad patch. The apparent return of confidence that had helped to underpin his performances at the Princes was no less apparent in the weeks on tour that followed. As one admiring reviewer wrote of his performance in *Ruddigore* in Bournemouth at the end of May:

> "That young [*sic*] stalwart of the D'Oyly Carte Company, Leonard Osborn, carried off the chief honours – in the first act at least – as the dashing Dick Dauntless. Greeted with a spontaneous round of applause, he made an explosive impact, bringing a salty breeze into the production. He projected his tenor voice to all parts of the theatre with ease, and quickly proved himself to be an actor of no mean ability.
>
> But it was his dancing of the hornpipe that made an outstanding impression. This was executed with a smooth fluency and grace rarely captured by a male dancer"

- all of which was particularly impressive considering that the previous week he'd been off with a severe attack of laryngitis.

Frederic Lloyd's prophecy the previous October – "I think that with careful handling we shall be able to get Mr Osborn through the London season" – had proved correct. They'd got him comfortably beyond it too. What was to say they wouldn't continue to handle him in the same way for another season, another two seasons, or even longer?

The answer came later that summer.

It was mid-August, during the Company's annual vacation. Bridget D'Oyly Carte had made a decision, and on the 18th Frederic Lloyd sent her the following memo relating to that decision:

> "I saw Mr Leonard Osborn today and told him that we should require him to leave the Company at the end of the season at Streatham Hill [in December]. He was extremely pleasant, and I think, although no doubt the news was naturally a shock to him, he was in a way half expecting it, as he was on a short-term contract.
>
> He did make one or two remarks about production which were not, I consider, in the best of taste, and I have already mentioned these to you. But there is no doubt that he was upset, and I think at the same time trying to impress me with what he could do.
>
> I think perhaps it might be as well if you would write him a letter on the lines of the draft attached?"

Bridget complied six days later.

> "Dear Mr Osborn
>
> "As Mr Lloyd I know has told you, I am intending to make a change in the Company, and this letter is therefore to confirm that I shall not require your services after the Company leave Streatham Hill Theatre on 19th December 1959.
>
> It may so happen that during the course of the next few months we shall require your successor to play some trial performances and I will, of course, notify you of these in due course.
>
> I should like to take this opportunity of telling you how much I appreciate all the work that you have done during the many years that you have been with us.
>
> We shall all miss you very much, I can assure you, but I believe that you will appreciate that from every point of view, your own as well as ours, this decision should be made now."

So it had happened. Happened when he must have felt he least deserved it, and even – whatever Frederic Lloyd may have thought – when he least expected it. For as Lloyd makes clear in his account of their meeting, the news came to him as a shock and that his reaction to it was one of genuine distress.

Yet how did this reaction tie up with his previously expressed readiness to go if and when he was asked to do so? The likeliest answer, it seems to me, is that subconsciously he had never expected that point to be reached; that as the months had gone by and his problems, at least since Christmas, had been resolved, he had convinced himself that, as there had been no further talk of his going up till then, there would be no further talk of it in the immediate future either.

But now there was no arguing. His time in the Company had been whittled down to just four more months, and this was a fact with which he had somehow to come to terms. And it was possibly resentment of that fact – a sudden urge, perhaps, to have done with the whole thing – that in an interview with Bridget on August 25th he seems to have suggested shortening that period still further. For on the 27th Bridget was writing to him again, and this time she said:

"Dear Mr Osborn

Subsequent to our talk on Tuesday, I find we can make it convenient for you to terminate your engagement on Saturday 31st October.

I had, however, overlooked the point that this date will cover the first week at Golders Green, and it may be that you would prefer to finish on the previous Saturday at Leeds? Perhaps you will let me know your decision on this matter."

Curiously, though, it was nearly a month before the date of his going was finally settled. This time (September 24th) it was Frederic Lloyd writing to him again:

"Mr Worsley has passed me your message, and I have told Miss D'Oyly Carte, who is very grateful to you.

We very much appreciate it that you will be prepared to sing while the Company is at Golders Green."

And what that meant was this: he would play the *whole* four week season at Golders Green, and officially leave the Company on that season's final Saturday, November 21st.

The news of his going, however, was not immediately made public. Instead it was kept under wraps for another month; that is, till near the end of October. The press release that announced the news was fairly short and fairly bland. But there was nothing bland about the reaction it produced among his D'Oyly Carte fans. From all sides came howls of dismay, disbelief almost amounting to a refusal to admit it was happening, and an accompanying feeling of hostility towards those who were thought to have brought it about.

Immediately a story circulated that he'd not just been asked to leave but had been sacked – sacked out of hand without warning and with, at most, four weeks notice. The most brutal version that gained currency had him learning of his dismissal from a letter which he found in his dressing room when he arrived to get ready for a performance. Another version had him first hearing of it from some unofficial source, the implication being that the management were too cowardly to tell him to his face. There were also suggestions that he'd previously been given hints he should go, and had had to be sacked in the end because he'd refused to take those hints.

But whatever precise form any of the stories took, they all added up to the same thing: the belief that he'd been treated appallingly, and that Bridget D'Oyly Carte, regarded as the culprit-in-chief, had handled the whole affair with a callous ruthlessness.

Yet as should be apparent from the letters and other communications I've quoted, this was an unhappy misunderstanding of what had actually occurred. Let's consider the situation again. The first intimation that he might be asked to leave had come in July 1958, a good fifteen months earlier. He was first told about the decision to release him not in a letter left in his dressing room or anywhere else, but by Frederic Lloyd in person. He was not given four weeks notice but four *months* which, if he was then on a short-term contract, was hardly unreasonable.

Knowing nothing of the real story at the time, I believed every alternative version I heard then and for some time afterwards. Like so many of his fans, I believed he'd been treated appallingly. But it's clear to me now that Bridget had a fair case.

Leonard, in the nature of things, would have to go sometime. Moreover, tenors in musical theatre have an in-built handicap: they are mostly required to play men who are young or are assumed to be young. As they grow older they inevitably begin to strain credibility in such roles, especially when playing young men *in love*; though that's not to say – far from it – that no D'Oyly Carte tenor had ever strained credibility in this respect before. Leonard was now approaching forty-five. He might get away with playing the character parts – Tolloller and the Duke of Dunstable – for some time to come, but how much longer could he go on convincingly playing Fairfax or "young Richard" - Dick Dauntless? – whatever that Bournemouth reviewer may have thought.

On the other hand, his acting and dancing skills were as good as ever. So were there parts other than those he was now playing that he might conceivably play instead? Back in October the previous year Billy Morgan, though dismissive of Leonard's future as a tenor, had come up with the idea that he might try switching to *baritone* roles. But Leonard, when he heard about this idea, would have nothing to do with it. As he once subsequently remarked: he had lived as a tenor and he would die as a tenor. However upsetting it might be, Bridget's conclusion that the time for him to go had arrived made sense. Furthermore, by going then (even though this wasn't a point she made herself) he would go at a time when he was still on top.

And having reached this conclusion, it's surely fair to say that she and Lloyd handled his dismissal at least as well as could be expected, and even with a fair degree of warmth. That sentence in her letter "We shall all miss you very much" was something she didn't *have* to say, and indeed was quite capable of *not* saying if she didn't want to. Frederic Lloyd's letter to him on the opposite page actually began with the words "Dear Leonard". Admittedly it wasn't quite the first time he (Lloyd) had begun a letter to him that way. But for the representative of an employer to address an adult employee by his Christian name in the 1950s was, if not totally unheard of, then certainly unusual, at any rate in so hierarchical an organisation as D'Oyly Carte, and in circumstances such as they were in that autumn of 1959.

But the trouble was, that constituted only one part of the story. It had another part too, and in many people's minds the two parts, unfortunately though not unsurprisingly, got mixed up. While there was now a reasonable case for asking Leonard to leave, there was an equal imperative to ensure that the person who replaced him was someone worthy of doing so.

There were, within the Company itself, at least three candidates for the job, one of these now being Thomas Round. Round, only a year younger than Leonard as previously mentioned, was also, as he realised himself, approaching the stage when he should no longer be playing clearly youthful parts like Ralph Rackstraw and Frederic. But he still had the looks and manner to suggest he might reasonably adapt to the more mature tenor parts, and vocally, as Leonard himself put it some time later, he "was able to look after his voice better than I looked after mine".

Then there were the two tenor understudies. One of these was John Fryatt, who covered for Leonard as Tolloller and the Duke. The other was Frederick Sinden. "Colonel Fairfax was played with commendable spirit by Frederick Sinden," a reviewer had written when Leonard was off in Bournemouth that May.

Yet Leonard's successor was to be none of these three, but a total newcomer. In itself this was nothing extraordinary. While the majority of D'Oyly Carte principals down the years started as choristers, there were usually at any given time others who had come in as principals straight away. Of those performers who were principals in the late 1950s, Jean Hindmarsh and Kenneth Sandford, for example, came into this category. The same had effectively applied back in the '40s with Thomas Round. Now it applied to the performer who was to take over from Leonard, a man named John Stoddart.

John Stoddart, then aged thirty-two, had a perfectly reputable background. He had begun his career as a schoolteacher in Wales. Then having given up teaching in favour of singing, he had appeared at Glyndebourne and sung at various festivals. And his life might have continued along those lines without interruption had he not, completely out of the blue, been taken up by Eleanor Evans.

Eleanor Evans (Mrs Fancourt), known to almost everyone by the apparently affectionate nickname of "Snookie", had ended her reign as D'Oyly Carte Stage Director after the Sadler's Wells season of 1953. Her reign had not been without its positive side, but it had also shown up the fact that as a director she had considerable deficiencies. An inflexible thinker of limited intellectual capacity, she was strong-willed, autocratic, and didn't like being crossed.

More harmful still, she was a person who had "favourites". And people who have favourites – especially perhaps people with power – tend to be suspicious of and hostile to other people outside their particular clique. One of those other people who at some stage had incurred her hostility was Martyn Green; and having taken against *him*, she had proceeded to take against those other

Frederick Sinden as Colonel Fairfax

members of the Company who were – or who she considered were – his particular friends. Among those friends, as mentioned on page 44, was Leonard; and Leonard once said to Frederick Sinden: "Snookie's awful to me because I'm pally with Martyn."

And despite the fact that she'd officially retired from the Company, she continued to be a powerful influence in the background. Newcomers who needed instruction in the D'Oyly Carte way of doing things were sent to her for initial training; among them Kenneth Sandford and Gillian Knight, the latter being the replacement for Ann Drummond-Grant.

Bridget D'Oyly Carte, having had no real preparation for the job when she took over the Company in 1948, came to depend considerably on Snookie for advice and support as another woman in what was predominantly a man's world. But if this was understandable, it also had its damaging side. And its damaging side was never more clearly demonstrated than in Snookie's advocacy of John Stoddart.

One day during the summer of 1959 she (Snookie) apparently came across the latter in a music studio in Oxford Street, decided he was a great "find" and that he must be drafted into D'Oyly Carte at the earliest opportunity. "He would be the ideal tenor to replace Mr Osborn," she told Bridget; and got not only Bridget to agree to the idea but presumably Herbert Newby, who had now become Stage Director, and Isidore Godfrey as well. The whole business seems to have been worked with considerable speed.

Stoddart had a first audition on July 17th. A "pleasant voice", says his audition record. Some time afterwards he was appointed a principal tenor, to start after the December season at Streatham Hill; and with a replacement lined up, that was why Leonard was asked to leave the Company that summer rather than at any time previously, and why the end of the Streatham Hill season was the original date suggested for his going.

But Stoddart's appointment, it may be said straight away, was a definite miscalculation, though it's fair to suggest that any newcomer placed in the situation as it stood would have faced a difficult task. D'Oyly Carte audiences were known for their dislike of change and a certain reluctance to accept any performer who was replacing one of their special favourites.

There were, though, two things that could to some extent smooth a new principal's path. It could help if he or she had been around for some time. This factor certainly helped John Reed, the performer chosen to replace Peter Pratt. Reed had been Pratt's understudy for eight years, during which time he'd become, so to speak, part of the D'Oyly Carte furniture, familiar to audiences and colleagues alike. It could equally help, however sad it might be in one sense, if the newcomer was replacing a person who had died or was too ill to continue. This was the case with Gillian Knight, who had already taken several steps towards being accepted because nothing could now bring back Ann Drummond-Grant.

Neither factor, though, applied in the case of John Stoddart when he was chosen to replace Leonard. He himself was unknown – and Leonard was still

John Stoddart as the Defendant

very much alive. The contrast between the two of them could not have been more glaring. From the start Stoddart failed to impress. He failed to impress his fellow performers at rehearsal. Not only did it emerge that he'd had no idea G&S contained any spoken dialogue, but his singing came across as lifeless. Though personable in appearance he was another tenor who was short in stature, and that didn't help either. Certain of his fellow performers resented him – resented the fact that he'd got the job. And if he aroused feelings of this sort among his colleagues, what sort of feelings would he arouse among his audiences?

None of this, it equally needs saying, was his fault, and there were many others in the Company who felt genuinely sorry for him. He had been thrust into an uncomfortable and embarrassing position that was not in any way of his own making. Moreover it was a worrying time for him personally. In July his small son had been knocked down and injured by a car, and this had resulted in his wife suffering a temporary breakdown.

Meanwhile the D'Oyly Carte autumn tour was proceeding along its scheduled course in the smoothly run fashion in which D'Oyly Carte tours nearly always proceeded. Leeds, already mentioned, was the tour's venue number six. But now the two week season in the Yorkshire city had come to an end. The Company were moving south to London and Golders Green to begin the season that was to be Leonard's last. And for the four weeks encompassed by that season, Golders Green Hippodrome became the centre of the whole D'Oyly Carte world.

If this was D'Oyly Carte going through a period of some upheaval, it wasn't the easiest of times for the Hippodrome itself. It had been losing audiences, and there was, or would be, talk of it closing down. That possibility, however, seemed ludicrous when set against the interest evoked by the D'Oyly Carte season and the corresponding demand for seats. The local paper published a photograph of part of the gallery queue one evening, a queue comprising goodness knew how many people snaking up and down the wide pavement outside, and it gave that photo the defiant caption: "Does This Look Like A Dying Theatre?"

During that season Leonard played Tolloller and Fairfax four times each, the Duke of Dunstable three times and Dick Dauntless twice, making thirteen performances in total. Against that he played Cyril not at all, simply because after its four outings at the Princes and a couple more in Manchester immediately following, *Princess Ida* had been dropped from the repertoire once again; and he missed out on one Tolloller because John Stoddart was asked to play the role as a trial performance. Each of those thirteen performances had its emotional moments, and emotion gathered pace as he played each of his four roles for the last time.

The first of these, on the third Wednesday of the season, was Dick Dauntless – *Ruddigore's* Dick Dauntless, the part which, above all others, he had made his own. That night he sang his last "Parley-voo", danced his last hornpipe. At the end of each D'Oyly Carte performance of *Ruddigore* it was

The gallery queue at Golders Green Hippodrome, November 14th 1959
(Photograph: *Hendon and Finchley Times*)

customary for all the principal characters, standing in a line, to drink a toast to each other; and on this occasion, recorded Graham Davis in the *Gilbert & Sullivan Journal*, Leonard "impulsively took a half-pace forward and drank to the audience – a gesture of gratitude for their loyal support".

His second "last performance" – or rather in this case performances (matinee and evening) - were as the Duke of Dunstable the following Saturday. I was there for the evening performance, the one that really counted. The previous evening I'd been at a performance of *The Mikado*, a benefit performance for Martyn Green who had lost a leg in a horrific accident in New York the week before. But that and Saturday night's *Patience* were the only performances I was able to get to that season. And just as, twelve years earlier, the Duke of Dunstable had been the first part I saw Leonard play, so now it was the last; and I'm convinced – I swear – he'd never played it better.

After the show a great bevy of his fans and admirers – including the group I'd been with at the Princes earlier that year, and who naturally were present in force on this occasion – gathered near the stage door on that stretch of pavement occupied earlier in the evening by the gallery queue. The atmosphere was both exhilarating – we'd just emerged from a wonderful performance – and yet, underneath, desperately, desperately sad. All of us in the group, I think, sensed – even if we didn't admit it openly – that we were coming to the end of an era; our own D'Oyly Carte era, that is, just as much as it was the end of an era for the Company itself.

Leonard's final performance as Fairfax was on the following Tuesday, November 17th. On the Thursday, a day he was not required on stage, Bridget D'Oyly Carte sent him a farewell letter that only added to the week's emotion. "We are going to miss you very much in the Company," she wrote once again, "and I do hope that you will keep in touch with us ... All my good wishes to you." To repeat the comment I made on page 101, she didn't have to say that, and there seems no reason to believe those wishes were not sincere.

There was now just one *day* to go. Leonard's final performance of all: Earl Tolloller on the Friday. And the fact that his final performance was to be on a Friday was another aspect of his going that gave rise to criticism. Surely, many people felt, the season's programme could have been rearranged so he could go out on an appropriately high note on the Saturday, the season's last night.

But this was another aspect of his going wherein criticism was misplaced. The programme would have been settled well before the time, scarcely two months earlier, that the date of his departure was finalised. Publicity had already been distributed. The box office had already started taking bookings for seats. To have changed the programme after it was announced would hardly have endeared the Company to the theatre management, and could have caused any amount of chaos, not to mention considerable additional expense.

So on that Friday evening, November 20th 1959, Leonard bowed out as Tolloller, the first major part in any of the full-length operas he had played in the Company, and in the same theatre in which he'd played it all those years before. The evening is described in all its desperate emotion by Rob Weston, another youthful enthusiast for whom Golders Green Hippodrome was the local theatre too:

"I and several of my fellow enthusiasts were determined to be there. We joined the queue early in the evening as we wanted to be in the front row of the gallery if possible. We were certainly near the front and very high up in the theatre. I remember the buzz that was so apparent as everyone wanted to say goodbye to their hero, and we waited impatiently for his first entrance. Suddenly he was on the stage and a burst of applause rang out."

But with that applause came, almost immediately, a huge feeling of disappointment for, as Weston remembers it, the action of the opera continued with scarcely a break:

"In our ignorance we had expected some immediate acknowledgment of Osborn's impending departure. Short bursts of applause followed his every action but were totally ignored by the rest of the cast and the Musical Director. During the interval we comforted ourselves with the sure knowledge that final curtain calls would send him on his way with our adulation ringing in his ears.

But it was not to be. The performance continued and ended as if this was just another evening in the routine of D'Oyly Carte – which, of course, it was. No individual curtain call, no special bow. The curtain came down and Leonard Osborn as a performer passed into history. I remember feeling so frustrated and let down."

The feeling of having been let down was totally understandable. But, as Weston later found out, it wasn't intended as a snub to Leonard, however much it seemed that way at the time. Rather it was simply a manifestation of the D'Oyly Carte ethos that no performer was bigger than the Company as a whole, and accordingly that no performer could be given any sort of preferential treatment – even though the rule *had* been broken in the past in the cases of Henry Lytton and Martyn Green.

As for Leonard's first entrance, it's interesting to compare Weston's description of it with the description penned by Graham Davis:

"The applause as [Osborn made that] entrance was tremendous and unmistakable in its affection. He could only stand with his head bowed in gratitude for some moments, before speaking his opening line."

Was there a wait of "some moments" before he spoke that line? Different people's perceptions of the same event will often vary. And the bowed head? Bowed in gratitude, yes; but bowed surely, too, in a struggle to contain his emotion. This he just about managed to do at that point and throughout the performance itself, though emotion was probably the cause of his getting a word wrong in a line in Act Two – something totally unlike him – and *after* the performance it overwhelmed him. Returning to his dressing room in what Frederick Sinden describes as "a terrible state", he broke down in uncontrolled tears.

109

Outwardly recovered, he emerged from the stage door into the crush of his fans, all there to get a last lingering sight of him. The "group", when they could get near him, handed him a farewell gift. What that gift was none of those I asked can remember now. But whatever it was, they had inscribed it with a quotation from one of the lines he had spoken so often as Colonel Fairfax:

"A Thousand Thanks, Good Sir."

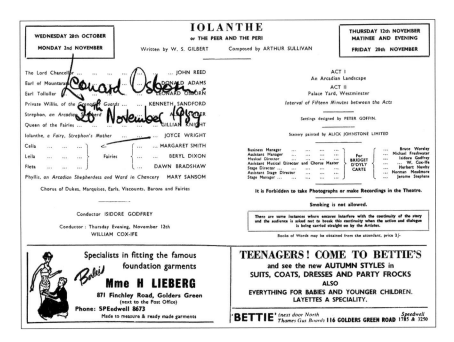

The programme for Leonard's final performance

"Obviously Enjoying It", 1960-76

He had been with D'Oyly Carte for twenty-two years, less approximately six years of the war, and for thirteen of those years he had been a principal tenor. It was an impressive record, and it looked even more impressive when set against the way things went with the Company's tenors in the wake of his departure. For within the next four years, no fewer than five principal tenors had played one or more of his five parts. Those five tenors included Thomas Round who at various times took over Fairfax, Dick Dauntless, Cyril, Tolloller and even the Defendant, and also sang Tolloller, Dick Dauntless and the Defendant on new recordings of *Iolanthe*, *Ruddigore* and *Trial by Jury*.

As for John Stoddart, he had lasted only a matter of months. Whatever Snookie had seen in him continued to escape everyone else. He "did not prove very satisfactory," as his Company card put it, and was "asked to leave" the following July. He was actually, it was noted, "quite pleased to do so", having realised that "his metier lay in oratorio and concert work".

Let's say it again. Leonard had been with D'Oyly Carte twenty-two years less approximately six years of the war – it was an impressive record. The emotional scenes which were part of his final season at Golders Green underlined just how much his performances during those years had meant to so many people. But now, on his departure from the Company, it quickly became clear that his long stay in just the one organisation had its downside.

For throughout that time he'd had little to worry about in the way of decision-making and organising his life. It wasn't that he was incapable of making decisions for himself. But essentially in D'Oyly Carte it was the management that made the decisions, and all *he* had to do in the Company was, in Tony Osborn's words, "sort out his own digs" – just as it had been the higher ranks that had made the decisions when he was in the RAF and "all he'd had to do then was his duty".

But now there were no equivalent higher ranks to make the decisions. Now he had to take full responsibility for his own life and, as one aspect of this, to start building himself a new career. It was something that was not going to be easy, given particularly that, at any rate at first, he had to do it in anything but the right frame of mind.

One of the many questions I asked Tony Osborn was, how did he (Leonard) feel about being pushed out of D'Oyly Carte? "Very cut up," was the answer. He felt hurt. He felt rejected. He felt totally lost, totally abandoned. Being Leonard, it seems hardly necessary to say, he never admitted this publicly. His D'Oyly Carte years, he had told a journalist when the news of his going was officially announced, had been good years, enriched and enlivened by warm friendships. But where could he find such friendships now? And who would now take him on and give him the new start he needed?

To begin with, he tried to find work as an actor, work for which he (Leonard) was still unquestionably fitted. But taken as a whole, the results were meagre. He fronted one or more advertisements on television. His picture, showing him holding a pair of spectacles in one hand and a phone to his ear in the other, appeared on a brochure advertising Telephone Rentals Services. He was once interviewed on radio by Brian Matthew. And he got a part in at least one television play.

I happened, partly by chance, to watch that play. I can't remember what it was called, but it was a courtroom drama. Leonard was cast as a junior counsel and had just two lines to speak; actually the same line twice: "My Lord, I must object!" Just the two lines. The camera was on him and off him in a matter of seconds. As with his final D'Oyly Carte performances it all seemed desperately sad.

With a further career in acting becoming less and less likely by the week, he eventually accepted he would have to look for something else. What he settled on was a job in the Croydon branch of the Advance Laundry.

Working in and for a laundry. A laundry might be a useful, even an essential, establishment, but could there be any establishment more prosaic, more mundane in which to spend one's days? It was hardly a place calculated to set the adrenalin flowing, and it gave him nothing like the satisfaction that G&S and the stage had done. Nonetheless he settled resolutely into its routine and coped with its demands, and at least it gave him job security and a regular income to bring home.

A regular income to bring home. Home since his re-marriage had been in Whyteleafe, a village to the south of Croydon in which his wife and their two boys had been living since 1949 or 1950. Despite his re-marriage it was inevitable that, while he was still in D'Oyly Carte and away week after week on tour, he had continued to spend little time at home. But now, with his touring days at an end, "little time" had become quite a *lot* of time, and his home situation wasn't all that happy either. If, in the words of Tony Osborn, he had hoped by his re-marriage to get back to a relationship that was "safe", safety had not yet brought a corresponding sense of ease and contentment. This wasn't necessarily surprising. He had the damage of more than ten years to repair.

Certainly Eileen, his wife, was happy to have him back. For her the intervening years had been years of considerable struggle. For a time she

TR INTERNAL BROADCASTING
will find him

With the introduction of SUBSCRIBER TRUNK
DIALLING (STD), the installation of TR Internal
Broadcasting becomes even more important.

If the wanted person cannot be located
immediately, he will be asked to "ring
back"—and you will bear the cost
of the call!

Leonard advertising Telephone Rentals Services
(D'Oyly Carte Opera Company Archive)

doubled up working for the local council, shepherding disabled children on part of their journeys to and from school with, for a time, a middle of the day job in a café. This was another café owned by Leonard's brother Frederick, a smaller one than its predecessor which he had given up after his mother stopped working. (Later he gave that one up too and, instead, opened a launderette. The launderette flourished just as the cafes had done, and in due course one launderette became several. It was almost as though laundry work ran in the family.)

But Eileen in those years had not only struggled financially. She had struggled emotionally too, trying to come to terms with life without the man she had married. Never a confident person, always (much like Leonard himself) somewhat insecure, she had idolised him from the word go. Despite all that had happened it was as though, in her eyes, he could still do no wrong. But for Tony and his brother, his renewed presence in their lives was nothing like so easy to adjust to. His own childhood had had its grim side. For them, if for different reasons, childhood had not been easy either.

There was no getting away from it. He had deserted them – had neither been around nor shown any interest in them – during their childhood, a time when they probably needed him most. This was particularly so in the case of Martin, the younger son, who had been born with what is now called cerebral palsy and needed a lot of help just getting through life from day to day.

Taken altogether, too much had happened – too many resentments had accumulated – for the two boys to forgive him quickly. Moreover around 1960, shortly after Leonard left D'Oyly Carte, misfortune befell Tony Osborn too. By then in his late teens, Tony was involved in a motor cycle accident, and was in hospital and various rehabilitation centres for about eight months. All this added – how could it not? – to the general atmosphere of strain.

Back to the laundry. For all his lack of enthusiasm for the job, Leonard obviously impressed his new employers with his capabilities, for in the summer of 1962 he gained promotion. This came in the form of a move from Croydon to take charge of a new branch of the laundry in the North London suburb of Finchley. With it came an income of more than a thousand a year, rising potentially to fifteen hundred, plus the prospect of a substantial pension at the age of sixty. Though even fifteen hundred a year was quite a bit less than he'd been getting during his last years with D'Oyly Carte, his future, in financial terms at least, had stabilised.

Yet if promotion gave him security financially, it didn't alter his feelings about the job itself. It was no good – he still wasn't *really* happy – still didn't really feel it was what he wanted to be doing. Nor in all probability did it help that he had to travel right across London to get to Finchley and back every working day.

And the upshot was that in April 1964, less than two years after the Finchley move, he changed tack once more, gave up the laundry and took over a shop. The shop was in Purley Oaks, one of Croydon's southern suburbs, and was a sub-post office and general store. Here he was certainly happier than he'd been in the laundry, later claiming that he'd made a lot of friends while he was there. Furthermore it was not just a shop but, with living quarters in the flat above, it became his and his family's new home. And one consequence of this was that he and Eileen ran the shop together.

That was a significant development. It was a mutual recognition that their life together was becoming re-established on a more relaxed and more settled footing, and this had a positive impact on the lives of their sons too. In April 1967 Tony Osborn got married. The wedding took place at Whyteleafe Parish Church and as part of the service Leonard sang a solo – the twenty-third psalm to the tune of *Crimond* – and by the time he finished, Tony says, "there wasn't a dry eye left in the building". Then in 1969 Martin emigrated to Australia, to begin a new life there.

The years passed. The 1960s merged into the 1970s. Leonard and Eileen were now in their mid-fifties. It seemed likely they would stay at the post office till their retirement. Yet if so they had reckoned without D'Oyly Carte. For long years in the past, D'Oyly Carte had been Leonard's life, and the time was approaching when it would become his life once more.

But that is to take the story too far ahead. Yet even though D'Oyly Carte wasn't the mainspring of his life for the moment, the same was not true of Gilbert and Sullivan. His continued involvement with G&S was ultimately what kept him going during these years. If he was no longer tied up with G&S professionally – no longer part of the theatre professionally – there was always the amateur theatrical scene.

The date was May 18th 1961, just eighteen months after his final D'Oyly Carte performances at Golders Green. That night he appeared in a leading role in the first of three or four performances of Cole Porter's *Kiss me Kate*. Those performances took place at the Scala Theatre, the same Scala Theatre in which he had appeared at the end of his first D'Oyly Carte tour, and were put on by the Advance Laundry Opera Company. What did I say about a laundry being a prosaic and mundane establishment? His performing credentials, or so he later claimed, were what had got him the laundry job in the first place.

But *Kiss me Kate* was only a start. A few months later he appeared in the laundry's production of *The Merry Widow* at the same theatre. In this he was cast as Danilo, the *Widow's* hero, and it was a casting not without irony: Thomas Round had been an enormous success in the part in a Sadler's Wells production of the same piece just three years before.

Then the following year (1962) he took part in a couple of productions mounted by the local Croydon Operatic and Dramatic Association (CODA). The first of these was *The Desert Song* and the second *The New Moon*, both of them pieces by Sigmund Romberg. "Leonard Osborn as the gallant Captain Fontaine is acceptably soldierly," pronounced the *Croydon Advertiser* of his showing in the first of these, though in one of the performances he endured a few moments of nothing less than torture. What happened is described by Ernie Thomas, then CODA's Assistant Stage Manager:

"Leonard as Captain Paul Fontaine was on stage when Lieutenant La Vergne should have entered. Unfortunately the actor playing that part was nowhere to be seen, and Leonard had to *ad lib* frantically until he eventually made his entrance with the immortal words: 'I'm sorry I'm late, sir. I was in the bar having a noggin'."

It was torture for Leonard because improvising and *ad libbing* was an aspect of stagecraft at which he admitted he was hopeless.

But acting was only one way – and very much the lesser way – that he became part of the amateur scene. There was also directing or, as it was then usually called, producing. Down the years any number of ex-D'Oyly Carte performers took up directing G&S and other works for amateur societies. And in 1963 Leonard became the latest of them to take up this form of involvement.

The idea of directing, indeed, had appealed to him for some time. It was partly the latent schoolmaster coming out in him; in a definite and possibly unusual way he equated directing with teaching. When back in 1951 he had written to warn Bridget D'Oyly Carte that the then circumstances of his private life might compel him to leave the Carte Company at short notice, he had mentioned significantly and without any prompting that he would be "only too pleased to help train the artist who will take my place" – in other words, teach the latter what to do. There had been the surreptitious teacher-to-pupil guidance he had given at different times to Frederick Sinden and Beryl Dixon.

There had also been an improbable press photograph taken in Los Angeles when the Company were in America in 1955, a photograph captioned "Beating the Heat", which showed him sitting in a swimming pool "directing" an impromptu rehearsal, with some of the other members of the Company sitting in the water with him as though they were a class of eager schoolchildren. Then, most significantly of all and while still a performer, he had indicated an interest in eventually becoming Stage Director of D'Oyly Carte itself.

Now between 1963 and 1976 he directed no fewer than twenty-eight productions for three amateur societies all in Surrey: the Opera Club of Reigate and Redhill; CODA, as mentioned above; and Godalming Operatic Society. Here is a list of those productions, arranged chronologically in each case:

For Reigate and Redhill:
The Mikado (1963); *Ruddigore*; *The Gondoliers*; *The Sorcerer*; *Iolanthe*; *Trial by Jury* and *HMS Pinafore*; *Princess Ida*; *The Pirates of Penzance*; *Patience*; *The Yeomen of the Guard*; *Ruddigore*; *The Gondoliers*; *The Mikado*; *Iolanthe* (1976)

For CODA:
The Gondoliers (1965); *Iolanthe*; *The Merry Widow*; *Trial by Jury* and *The Pirates of Penzance*; *The Yeomen of the Guard*; *The Mikado* (1972)

For Godalming:
The Gondoliers (1969); *The Pirates of Penzance*; *Princess Ida*; *The Yeomen of the Guard*; *Patience*; *The Mikado*; *Ruddigore* (the Society's Golden Jubilee Production); *Iolanthe* (1976)

116

Leonard as Captain Paul Fontaine in *The Desert Song*
(Photograph: Studio Cole, New Morden)

It was a considerable workload; and in two of those productions he took a part as well: in CODA's *Gondoliers* when, intriguingly, he played Luiz, and in the first of Reigate's two *Iolanthes,* when he rolled back the years by once more playing Tolloller.

So what particular attributes did he bring to the task of directing? The first of them was a total belief in G&S as a form of entertainment. As he told a later interviewer: "There is so much fun in [the operas], so much humour. They contain no message. They are sheer entertainment." And wasn't that "sheer entertainment" supremely worthwhile?

His productions of the operas were all "traditional". It didn't matter which of them he was engaged on, his aim in effect was to re-create the D'Oyly Carte production as he had known it. In going for the traditional, though, he was far from being alone. Almost every ex-D'Oyly Carte performer who went into directing amateur productions took the same line. But while many of them did so without giving the question any real thought, Leonard – and this was the second attribute he brought to his directing role – gave it a great deal of thought, just as previously he had always given thought to what he did as an actor.

And unlike many traditionalists – with the name of Snookie Fancourt immediately springing to mind as a prime example – his thinking on the subject was not totally rigid. As an instance of this, he cited a production of *The Mikado* in which he radically altered the character of Pooh-Bah:

> "Pooh-Bah ... is usually a large and pompous old man. But in [this production] the only chap who was suitable vocally was twenty-three and slim. So I dressed him as a young man and adapted the characterisation to make him very public school, straight out of Eton [or] Winchester ... and it worked."

Even more strikingly, when one of his performers (Reg Brown of CODA) mentioned hearing of a production of *Princess Ida* set in a South American jungle, and asked him what he thought about this, Leonard came out with a surprising answer: he wouldn't do such a production himself, but he was not averse to anybody else doing it – provided the key to the show was still Gilbert.

A third attribute, and perhaps the most important attribute of all, that he brought to directing was his own personality – himself. Leonard the director of amateur productions was like Leonard at the D'Oyly Carte stage door writ large: a warm, smiling personality who always looked pleased to see the people around him. At the stage door he was a star, and in the world of amateur operatics he was a star too – though this, as with the "traditional" aspect of his productions, was not something unique to *him*. So, to his or her own particular following, was every other D'Oyly Carte performer who ventured on to the amateur scene.

But Leonard was not only a star. No less to the point, his D'Oyly Carte status and background gave him total authority, and thanks at least in part to having that authority, he was totally in his element. This was something else about him that Barry Pendry, the graphologist, deduced from his handwriting.

He was only happy when he could "dominate his surroundings and the people involved, due to a flaw in his self-confidence," as Pendry puts it – though this suggests a certain arrogance and insensitivity that nobody in the amateur operatic world would have recognised even for a minute. Rather he gained the complete and unstinted admiration and respect of everyone in that world with whom he came into contact.

He worked his amateur groups hard; was completely professional in his approach to rehearsals – everything and everybody (though perhaps especially the tenors) had to be "just so". But he made those rehearsals enjoyable too. He never shouted or lost his temper. He explained things clearly and without wasting words. He was always generous with advice on any aspect of stagecraft, and particularly on characterisation. He made it abundantly and reassuringly clear that he knew what he was doing and, almost as important, why he was doing it, which is not the case with every stage director. Furthermore

> "he could act any of us, male or female, off the stage, and if he wanted a particular style which we weren't grasping, he would ask us to stand out front and watch him acting the part or scene in question"
>
> (Janet Hazell, Reigate and Redhill)

while David Longes, also of Reigate, recalls a piece of advice Leonard gave him when he was playing Ko-Ko during the run of their second *Mikado*:

> "During the interval one night, after the orchestra had had their fill of the sandwiches that were provided, the cast promptly descended on what was left. Leonard was in the men's dressing room at that moment, and I happened to remark that I couldn't eat prior to an evening show, but that once we had started I felt ravenous. Leonard said I should really eat before the show, because it gave the body the necessary energy – and Ko-Ko was certainly an energetic part.
>
> I said that I couldn't eat beforehand because it made me feel sick, and I've always remembered Leonard's reply: 'An empty drum makes a lot of noise, but not necessarily a good sound'."

And as well as respect and admiration he won their hearts. "Both my late husband and I had the pleasure of working with Leonard and remember him with the greatest affection," writes Jean Pratt of Godalming. "He was a delightful person, shy and unassuming," say various other participants in his productions to whom I've spoken, and he was always considerate to everyone around him. This is Ian Van Ryne, Reigate and Redhill's Stage Manager:

> "My most notable memory of Leonard is that he was the only producer/director I worked with who always came up to me at the end of the dress rehearsal and said 'It's all over to you now, Van'. Any time after that that he wanted to go on stage to speak to anyone, he would come and ask permission first."

And with consideration went kindness and generosity. He sent one member of the Reigate group a personal get-well card when she had to miss a number of rehearsals. "We always wanted to please him," writes Janet Hazell; and once

> "after a less than successful dress rehearsal, he gave us notes, and realised that we were all very downcast, as we felt we had let him down. On the first night he brought along an enormous tin of chocolates to cheer us up."

Nor was his sense of humour dormant for long. This is Janet Guppy of CODA:

> "I once took two acquaintances to a performance of *Pirates* by Reigate and Redhill. Neither of them had ever indicated any liking for Gilbert and Sullivan, but I thought they might be interested. I sat between them, and at one point they both fell sound asleep. Leonard, sitting behind us, tapped me on the shoulder and said, smiling: 'Your friends are obviously enjoying it'!"

And Leonard was obviously enjoying it too – enjoying the whole experience of working with amateur groups – and he could probably have gone on directing such groups for a considerably longer time than he did. But in 1976 something happened that led him to call a halt.

It's time now to get back to Leonard and D'Oyly Carte.

The bitterness and unhappiness he'd felt that night in 1959 – that night at Golders Green Hippodrome after his final *Iolanthe* – could have lasted years. It could have stayed with him for the rest of his life. But however overwhelming it had seemed at the time, he got over it remarkably quickly. According to Frederick Sinden, his bitterness was directed not at Bridget D'Oyly Carte but at Snookie Fancourt on whose machinations he, fairly or unfairly, blamed his dismissal.

In the years after he'd gone, however, her input on D'Oyly Carte matters seems eventually to have declined; and it was surely an indication of goodwill on both sides that by November 1960, exactly a year after he left the Company and during his early "laundry" days, he was on its payroll again. Not now as a performer. Not as a director/producer. But working at home preparing/writing prompt books for the various operas in the D'Oyly Carte repertoire.

Whether he was asked if he'd like to do this, or whether the initiative came from himself, isn't clear. If he was asked, the most likely person to have asked him was Frederic Lloyd. But whichever way it was, he was taken on; and once he'd done a first couple of books to get into the swing of it, a routine was established: the D'Oyly Carte office would send him six more books to work on at a time – two each of three operas. The rate of pay was one pound ten shillings per completed book unless it was *The Gondoliers* or *Patience*, each of

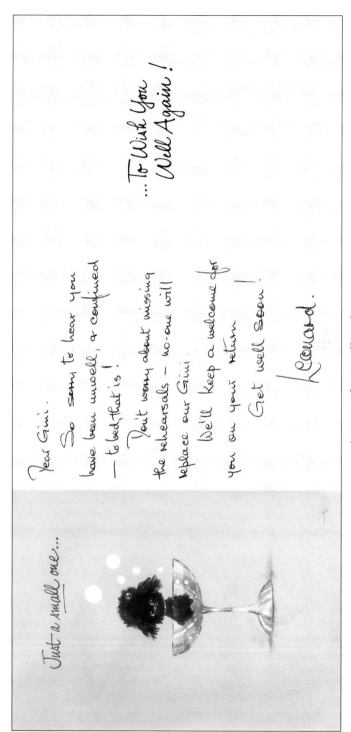

A personal get-well card

121

which for some reason qualified for two pounds, or *Trial by Jury*, when it was only a pound.

His detailed knowledge of the D'Oyly Carte productions chimed in well with all this. And his pleasure at doing it is evident from a letter he wrote to the office staff in January 1961, a letter which opened with the jaunty greeting "Hallo, Girls!"

> "Here are three *Yeomen of the Guard* and the Copy Book. That leaves me with one *Yeomen* and two *Ruddigore* to do.
>
> As you say, I don't have so much time to do them, but I would like to continue doing them – laundering doesn't pay all that well. I can manage one a week (I think) or maybe two in three weeks.
>
> All best wishes. God bless!
>
> Leonard."

Then on December 30th that same year, 1961, as though to indicate that his renewed contact with the Company amounted to more than a series of private communications with the office he (as it were) went public. That night saw the last performance of a G&S opera before the copyright on Gilbert's libretti ran out, and D'Oyly Carte lost their monopoly hold on the operas in Britain. That performance took place at the Savoy Theatre as part of the Company's winter season that year. The opera presented was *Princess Ida*. And to mark the occasion, a number of past D'Oyly Carte performers were there in the audience. Those performers included John Dean, Derek Oldham, Leslie Rands and Marjorie Eyre. And Leonard.

If these were the beginnings of Leonard's readmission to the D'Oyly Carte fold, his full public return – or reconciliation with the Company, as it must have appeared to many of his fans – may be said to have dated from January 1966 when the *Savoyard*, since 1962 the Company's house magazine, featured him in a short piece in an ongoing series of "Old Favourites".

The piece began by referring to the effect he had always had on the opposite sex. " 'Leonard, my loved one, come to me ... my heart is thine for aye.' How many feminine hearts," demanded the writer, "must have echoed Elsie Maynard's words in the years 1937-1959?" There was a mention of his stage entrances and the encores he got for his *Ruddigore* hornpipe; and then came a reference to his departure from the Company, which was surely an example of what would now be called spin. "When he left in 1959 to go into business, he was at the height of his popularity [and was] greatly missed". A decision to "go into business" was certainly not the reason he'd left. But one purpose of the *Savoyard* was to peddle the official line on whatever issues – and concerning whatever people - an official line was thought necessary; and it may reasonably be taken that his "business" activities had become the official line on Leonard.

He was also present in the audience on at least four more D'Oyly Carte London occasions during these years: one first night and three last nights. And while none of the first three of these occasions saw his presence in the theatre being obviously trumpeted, it was a different matter with the fourth one. The date of that fourth occasion was April 5th 1975, the theatre was the Savoy again, and it was the Last Night of what was called the D'Oyly Carte Centenary Season. Theoretically the main item on the bill that night was a concert performance of the final G&S opera, *The Grand Duke*. But what most people who were there principally remember about it are the proceedings before, and the performance of, *Trial by Jury* that followed.

First a line-up of no fewer than fourteen former D'Oyly Carte figures came on stage in evening dress to be presented to the audience in ones and twos. And among those fourteen were Ella Halman and Radley Flynn, Jeffrey Skitch – and Leonard, who came on with Cynthia Morey. All of them were received with rapturous applause. And when at last *Trial by Jury* itself got under way, they all took part in the performance as members of the chorus, vigorously singing the familiar words and music as though they'd never been away from D'Oyly Carte at all.

It was a performance of unbridled nostalgia, and after it was over Joan Robertson, mentioned earlier in this book as Frederic Lloyd's secretary, went over to a group of fans who had been in the audience and, with shining eyes, said "Did you see my Leonard?" Re-read that question word by word. Can there be any doubt that he was once again a fully paid-up member of the D'Oyly Carte family, and that there were still any number of people around who took a keen proprietary interest in him?

In fact it's likely that in the intervening years he and Joan Robertson had never totally lost touch, if only because he'd kept in some sort of touch with Frederic Lloyd. Back in December 1971 there had been a charity concert at the Redbridge Town Hall, Ilford to celebrate the centenary of the first Gilbert and Sullivan opera, *Thespis*. The concert was given by a choir conducted by the ex-D'Oyly Carte bass Ivor Evans. Frederic Lloyd, as chairman of one of the three charities concerned, was guest of honour. Leonard was there as the evening's "raconteur".

But if there was nothing inherently surprising in that, what happened just over three years later might be termed a surprise of the first order. On January 13th or 14th 1975 Leonard went to a D'Oyly Carte performance of *Princess Ida* during the Company's winter season at Sadler's Wells which immediately preceded the Savoy Centenary Season. This was apparently at the request of Frederic Lloyd, who asked him to write a report giving his impressions of the production.

And whether what he wrote was what Lloyd wanted to read, he certainly didn't mince his words. His overall impression of that *Ida* had been considerably less than favourable. His criticisms, expressed partly in note form, were blunt and, in places, merciless. Here are just a few of them:

"The production appears to have lost all charm and magic. Chorus grouping[s] no longer mean anything, nor have they any meaning to the chorus who appeared glum and amateur [and seemed to have] no involvement in the action of the story.

With the exception of Mr Sandford [Kenneth Sandford, still King Hildebrand] and Miss Masterson [Valerie Masterson – Ida herself] none of the principals [were] particularly impressive.

Act Two: Ladies' students' gowns far too short. Their sandals, essential for Act Three, therefore exposed and most unsatisfactory … Groupings for various sections dull … Towards the end of act no sense of mounting tension and defiance.

I would like to see more 'togetherness' from the three [young men] – Hilarion, Cyril and Florian – playing for each other, to each other; more fun, more panache. Florian and Cyril, the courtiers, eager to assist Hilarion in the escapade, Hilarion to be more dominant. He is the Prince, apparently the King's only son. His first entrance scarcely suggested a young prince eager to meet the child bride of twenty years ago.

Cyril's fun when he gets tipsy must be infectious. The character must have a little more abandon. Cyril and Florian … need more 'devil' in the[ir] characters."

And going back to the production as a whole:

"There was no JOIE."

Little more than eighteen months later Leonard was invited by Bridget to re-stage the Company's production of *Princess Ida* himself.

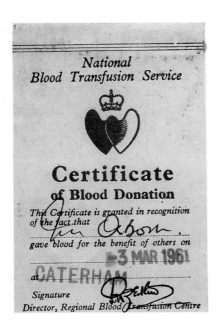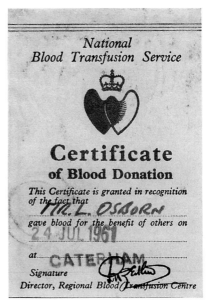

Leonard as a blood donor
(David Mackie collection)

"Lips, Tongue and Teeth", 1976-80

Invited by Bridget to re-stage *Princess Ida*.

This, remember, was the man who was supposed to have been sacked without warning by Bridget in 1959. But even allowing for the fact that was not what had actually happened, it was still a remarkable turnabout. As for Leonard himself, it didn't take him long to decide how to respond to the invitation. The chance to produce G&S professionally, the chance that he'd hankered after for so long, had come his way at last. "D'Oyly Carte," he later said, "is in my bloodstream." How could he not have returned to the Company when invited to do so? It would be wonderful to be back. He accepted the offer without hesitation.

Moreover, though getting him to re-stage *Princess Ida* was her first concern, it soon emerged that Bridget (*Dame* Bridget by now) wanted him to return to the Company as producer full time. In September 1976, clearly at her behest, Frederic Lloyd had a long talk with him about his personal life and future, explaining in the course of this what the Company were prepared to offer him; and a day or two later he was reporting back:

> "I suggested that for the production of *Princess Ida* we should probably be thinking in terms of a fee of five hundred pounds. He gets about two hundred and fifty [to] three hundred pounds for amateur productions, so I think this would be reasonable.
>
> We talked about the possible sale of his business should he decide to come to us permanently because, as we do not want him to be out of pocket at all, we must know how much he can expect from this. I was a little taken aback when, in talking about the business, I discovered that his salary as postmaster is now a minimum of five thousand pounds a year (a hundred pounds a week), added to which he gets approximately two thousand pounds a year (forty pounds a week) clear from the shop.
>
> I think, therefore, we have got to do some very careful thinking, as our present producer's total salary, including subsistence, is only ninety pounds a week. I am not at all certain that Mr Osborn, at the age of sixty-one, would want to drop that amount of income, nor do I think he

should be expected to do so unless he were able to sell his business for a considerable sum and invest the proceeds.

Also, at present he and his wife live over the shop, which would mean he would have to find alternative accommodation, as Mrs Osborn would not be prepared to tour.

There is no doubt that he would dearly love to take on the work of our permanent producer, but we have got to face these problems."

For several months the situation remained largely unresolved. But Leonard could live with things being like that for the moment – that is, while he was concentrating solely on *Princess Ida*. And already preparations for *Ida* were under way. The opera was to be given seven performances during the latter part of the Company's forthcoming new season at Sadler's Wells. Leonard would start rehearsals in January (1977), holding them each Tuesday and Thursday morning; and on February 17th his re-staged production had its first night.

But how was it received? London newspapers and magazines rarely gave D'Oyly Carte performances rave reviews in the 1970s. Leonard's *Princess Ida* immediately bucked this trend, at any rate so far as the *Evening News* and the magazine *Time Out* were concerned.

Said the *Evening News*:

"Producer Leonard Osborn has adroitly moulded text to contemporary tastes without sacrificing any of the traditional flavour. [The whole opera] bowls along with a robust assurance of both its musical and comic values. The Company settled into it with the enthusiasm of committed activists and there was some particularly fervent chorus work."

While as *Time Out* put it:

"Unjustly neglected, *Ida* should with a little more exposure take its place in the G&S Top Three ... Given the present distinguished attention and preparation, *Ida* should rule OK."

And, impressively, the opera took more money per performance than any of the other operas that season except *The Mikado* and the double bill of *Cox and Box* and *The Pirates of Penzance*. Moreover, if Leonard's production won plaudits from the D'Oyly Carte audiences in general, there is little doubt it pleased most G&S purists too; and after Sadler's Wells *Princess Ida* took its place, where physically practical, in the repertoire of the Company's provincial tour that followed.

One of the things that particularly pleased the purists was Leonard's decision to reinstate a number of dialogue cuts that had been made when the opera was revived in 1954. And this reinstating of *dialogue* having won approval, a musical number that had been cut as far back as the 1920s was in due course reinstated too. But this was a reinstating that in one quarter – and a

126

Leonard talking to Alison Cooper of the Opera Club of Reigate and Redhill, with Eileen Osborn sitting listening, after a performance of *Princess Ida* at Sadler's Wells

supremely important quarter at that – didn't go down well at all. What happened is related by David Mackie, the Company's Associate Conductor:

> "I think it was those of us on the production staff out on tour (I can't remember which of us it was for certain – it may have been Leonard's own suggestion) who decided to put back Lady Blanche's deleted song 'Come, Mighty Must'. I had the pleasure of conducting the song at one matinee at least. But we had omitted to tell the London office, and when word got back to them you could almost hear its foundations shaking, and Bridget's voice thundering 'Take that number OUT' "

and Leonard had to tell the Musical Director and the cast that he'd had a directive: "It's got to go." So it went. But Bridget must in due course have had second thoughts about it, for it was again reinstated when the opera was performed during the Sadler's Wells winter season of 1977-78.

Reverting, though, to the previous Wells season ... With a successful *Princess Ida* under his belt, the way had opened for Leonard to sort things out with regard to his shop, and step up to the official status of D'Oyly Carte Director of Productions on the permanent basis that Bridget wanted. But sorting out the shop – that is, getting it off his hands – was easier said than done. During the period he was rehearsing *Ida* he had drafted in an assistant to help keep things going those days he was at the theatre. But this was a temporary arrangement at best and wasn't the main problem anyway. On April 14th 1977 Frederic Lloyd had alerted Bridget to a very gloomy scenario:

> "I telephoned Leonard Osborn yesterday" (*wrote Lloyd*) "to find out the position regarding his future, and discovered he was in the depths of depression.
>
> The chances of his selling the business seem to be very vague. There is one man slightly interested who has put up some money to the agent handling the sale, but no more than that.
>
> He gave in his official notice to the Post Office at the beginning of the year and officially ceased to be Postmaster in March, but in view of the situation they have extended his service ..."

Yet in the event all the gloom proved unnecessary. A month later everything was settled. He'd got the business off his hands after all. He and Eileen moved out of the attached flat to a flat in nearby Sutton. And on May 16th he took up the appointment of D'Oyly Carte Director of Productions at ninety pounds, plus thirty pounds subsistence, a week. There was no talk of any depression now. Back in January, after he'd embarked on *Princess Ida*, a local paper, the *Coulsdon and Purley Advertiser*, had published an article about him with the pungently rhyming title

"No More Stamping Letters – It's Back to Operettas!"
"Sub-Postmaster Returns to D'Oyly Carte"

There was also, in the body of the article, a quote from his wife. Producing G&S for D'Oyly Carte was "something Leonard has always wanted to do", said Mrs Eileen Osborn.

And now he was doing it. He called the period he'd been away his "seventeen year sabbatical". The *Savoyard* that May, in alluding to his return, informed its readers that he'd been "one of the most popular tenors in the whole history of the Company" and that it was "with great delight that he is now welcomed back as producer". He himself was full of hope, of bubbling anticipation of what he might achieve in the months and years ahead.

Nonetheless his return did raise a few eyebrows, and one person who almost certainly wasn't too happy to see him walk back in as he did was the man whose job he had taken over. This was Michael Heyland, who had been Director of Productions since 1970. In 1971 Heyland had been responsible for producing *The Sorcerer* for its first revival since the war, and had done so to considerable acclaim. Four years later he did even better by producing *Utopia Limited*, the first time the Company had performed this opera since the beginning of the century.

He undoubtedly got a suspicion that something involving Leonard was going on at the time of the latter's report-writing visit to *Princess Ida* earlier that same year. It may be he came to feel that Bridget's and Lloyd's cosying up to Leonard meant that he (Heyland) was about to be sidelined. At all events, either in late 1976 or early 1977 he put in his resignation and left the Company that February, though he did return on three later occasions to direct specific productions.

Leonard had a clear idea what his role as Production Director should be. Essentially it was to oversee, to tidy and tighten up, the Company's productions already established rather than come up with new productions himself; and in this limited respect he believed he could make a real difference. He was confident of his strengths, but equally he realised his limitations. "I have the humility to know that I am not a creative producer of shows," he told one interviewer. "But I can teach character-playing, how it should be done, and style." And there again was that word "teach", and what teaching, to him, implied. In his producing role he saw himself as very much an authority figure.

As part of this role he had to work in tandem with James Marsland. James ("Jimmy" as he was always known) Marsland, two years his senior, had joined the Company as a chorister in 1949. The highest he rose as a performer was to play Annibale in *The Gondoliers* (three short dialogue speeches; no solo singing) at various times in the 1950s, and to call his performances in the part expressionless was almost an understatement. In 1966, however, he switched from being a performer to the production side of things, and it was immediately clear that by doing so he had found his true vocation.

If Leonard was the authority figure, Jimmy Marsland was the workhorse. It was his job to coach newcomers to the Company in all their actions and moves. And he loved it. No workhorse was ever more willing to work and, knowing every word and every note of every song, he would join in merrily with the singer or singers he was working with and rehearsing at any time. "When I do a rehearsal," he told a journalist in 1979, "I am like a long-playing record." Not surprisingly, therefore, he was regarded by most people in the D'Oyly Carte world as a Company treasure.

As may be seen from those glimpses in the previous chapter of Leonard's time with his amateur societies, there are in essence two main sides to the work of a stage director. On the one hand there's the artistic side: the way a director sees a production or, in the case of D'Oyly Carte, a *group* of productions; while along with this there's the personal side, dealing with the performers and other people who have the task of putting his ideas across in actual performance. And to be fully successful, a director needs to be effective on both counts.

On the first, the artistic side, Leonard scored ... brilliantly? No. But let's say reasonably well. He made a point now and again of watching performances from out front, something that not all his predecessors had done. He also had his fixations and his quirks. But what stage director hasn't?

One of those fixations – impressed on him back in the 1930s by J.M. Gordon as one of Gilbert's own fixations – was the absolute importance of good diction. "Lips, tongue and teeth" were the crucial elements in this – that was his dictum: "Lips, tongue and teeth". During his period as Production Director the Company went on two more tours abroad: another visit to America in 1978 and a first ever tour of Australia and New Zealand in 1979. And on the subject of diction an Australian journalist recorded a delightful interjection he addressed to the ladies' chorus during a rehearsal of *Iolanthe* in Canberra:

" 'Darlings!' came a beautifully modulated voice from the darkness of the stalls. The word tripping must not sound like dripping'."

And he certainly achieved something in this respect. Praise came from a number of quarters. The general word clarity of the chorus was "outstanding", wrote the *West Australian* of a performance of *HMS Pinafore* in Perth. "It was a pleasure to hear people on the stage who opened their mouths both to sing and to speak," cooed the Wellington (New Zealand) *Evening Post* of a performance of *The Mikado.* "Words became articulate."

While in terms of his productions as a whole:

"I fancy I see the hand of that old Savoyard Leonard Osborn ... in some minor but effective adjustments of movement and grouping" (wrote a Manchester journalist reviewing a performance of *Pirates* in 1979). "I would like to see a little less rapid delivery of the spoken word in Act One. But perhaps that is nit-picking, for the *Pirates* is really great entertainment and this Company is bang on form."

Moreover, as has also been mentioned in connection with his amateur productions, his approach to G&S was not totally inflexible, nor was he against change automatically. He had seen enough changes in the D'Oyly Carte productions in his own time to realise that a certain flexibility in performance was important, that within the overall framework of a production a performer's own personality had "got to shine through". After all, *his* own personality had always shone through in his performances, and had done so to tremendous effect.

Inevitably, of course, his efforts were sometimes met not with praise but with criticism; and here is another notice relating to his *Pirates*, one that appeared in the *Boston* (USA) *Globe,* and in this case a notice in which praise and criticism were oddly welded together:

> "Too many important moments ... are botched in this production. The whole encounter between pirates and police in the second act, for example, is most clumsily staged, with everyone bunched in the corners of the set. But Leonard Osborn, the producer, saw to it that everyone went through the most pointless and muddled business with great energy, brightness and professionalism."

But as well as overseeing the operas individually, there was another aspect of the Company's performances with which he had to get to grips, and that was the question of the Last Nights of the annual seasons at Sadler's Wells. These Last Nights owed much of their impetus to that hilarious *Trial by Jury* that had rounded off the Princes season in 1959 – the *Trial by Jury* in which Leonard and Donald Adams had shared a copy of *Lady Chatterley's Lover.*

Yet by comparison with that occasion, what was now happening on these occasions was, as often as not, positively over the top. Now, instead of the Company letting their hair down for just one part of the performance, they were letting it down for the whole evening. And, in the process, the result had at times become distinctly tacky.

The Last Night in February 1977, for instance, was theoretically given over to a performance of *HMS Pinafore*. But it was *Pinafore* with items from several of the other operas inserted, as well as a number of very un-G&S-like and dubious deviations, not to mention a cringe-making moment just before the end when, as the *Gilbert & Sullivan Journal* described it,

> "Michael Heyland unexpectedly pressed a plate of gooey cream into John Reed's face [and he] in turn pressed the plate with the remainder of the cream into the face of Royston Nash, the Musical Director."

Leonard that night had been in the audience – it was just after the initial performances of his *Princess Ida* and before he rejoined the Company on a permanent basis. And when in due course the time came round to start considering the programme for the next (February 1978) Last Night, he made his views clear to Frederic Lloyd:

> "Leonard Osborn feels very strongly that he wants to get as far away as possible from the over-playing and vulgarity of the Last Night in 1977" (*Lloyd informed Bridget and others*) "and has suggested we should have the first act of *Pirates of Penzance* played straight as far as possible, and that the rest of the evening should be designed entirely on the lines of a

131

concert, which we have done before, and run on the lines of a Victorian Music Hall, with the whole Company in suitable costumes."

And he was not alone in his feeling. Bridget's feeling about the content of recent Last Nights clearly reinforced the conclusion he'd come to himself. "Dear Mr Osborn," she eventually wrote to him when the 1978 Last Night was less than a month away,

> "As the Last Night has rather got out of hand in the last few years, I would be glad if you would please let the members of the Company know that I do not wish any extra 'business' to be inserted this year that has not previously been discussed and rehearsed with yourself."

So what was the programme actually played on that Last Night? The first act was indeed the first act of *The Pirates of Penzance* as Leonard had suggested. But to say it was *Pirates* played straight would have been stretching a point, to put it no higher. The only part of the proceedings that *was* played straight (or more or less) was the middle act, which was a performance of *Cox and Box*. The other two acts incorporated any number of what might best be called "turns". The performers, as in 1959, all appeared in the wrong costumes for what they were doing. And of a Victorian Music Hall there was no sign.

But thankfully there was no sign of any gooey cream either; and arguably the best turn of the evening was the first Patience-Grosvenor scene from *Patience* played by Barbara Lilley, one of the principal sopranos, and Kenneth Sandford as though they were performers in a not very slick amateur company.

They spoke the dialogue in unself-conscious north country accents. When Grosvenor (Sandford) was about to step on to the small coffin-like block on which, in the then D'Oyly Carte production, he stood to make one of his speeches, he suddenly realised it wasn't there, and let out a very unprofessional and deliberately unguarded aside. The orchestra wasn't ready at the end of the scene, and he had to repeat his final words of dialogue to cover the accidental-deliberate gap.

Whatever gave Leonard the idea (if it *was* his idea) for all that?

But while Leonard scored considerably as Stage Director in terms of thinking about what he was doing – while he had a clear conception of how he wanted things to be – the artistic side of the job – it was a different matter when he was dealing with the other people involved. In this respect he scored nothing like so well. To understand why that was so, it's necessary to mention who some of those other people were.

The first point to make here is that, while D'Oyly Carte was still D'Oyly Carte, it was almost as though in some ways he'd come back to a completely new Company. For of the fifty or so performers who had been around when he'd left in 1959, just four remained in residence as performers.

The most prominent of those four was John Reed, who had only just taken over the patter roles when Leonard left, but who was now a seasoned veteran. Second was Kenneth Sandford in the "Pooh-Bah" roles, an established veteran likewise; and both of them, naturally, had developed their own ways of doing things. Third was Jon Ellison, who had progressed from being purely a chorister to one who played small but important parts such as Bill Bobstay and Samuel. Fourth was Beti Lloyd-Jones, another small part player, chorister and understudy.

And just as Leonard would have remembered those four from the past, so each of those four would have remembered *him* and formed their impressions of him in the process. Beti Lloyd-Jones, for instance, had retained great admiration for him as an artist, while Kenneth Sandford was another person who had then thought him aloof – not that he (Sandford) wasn't prone to a certain aloofness himself. But to all the rest of the cast he was no more than a name. Most of them probably knew him by sight. Several of them may have come to know of his reputation as a performer. But none of them knew him as a colleague or in any way as a person, which meant in effect that he was a newcomer, to be regarded initially, perhaps, with a degree of caution. So how did he measure up?

On the positive side there were people who took to him immediately. One of these was David Mackie, who recounts an occasion on the American trip when

> "he showed me the centre of Washington DC. We walked from our hotel on a beautiful sunny morning to the Capitol – about five miles there and back.
>
> It was my first visit to America and I was grateful for his kindness. But we did get on well together, sharing among other things a liking for the *Telegraph* crossword."

Then there was Patricia Leonard, who became principal contralto in the summer of 1977, having previously been one of the soubrettes. She particularly remembers Leonard rehearsing her as Mad Margaret, and finding him during those rehearsals "very patient, charming and helpful". She also has a rehearsal story about her husband, Michael Buchan, who was also in the Company. It was *Princess Ida* and

> "Mike recalls making his first appearance as Arac (he was understudy) dressed from head to toe in heavy armour. Having got through Act One, he climbed three flights of stairs to his dressing room, only to hear his name being called back to the stage by Leonard to run through Acts Two and Three. He glanced sorrowfully at his cup of tea and clanked slowly back down."

Then, too, there was Jon Ellison, remembering him from earlier times. On the one hand Ellison's verdict on him concurs with that of Patricia Leonard. "When he returned to the Company as Stage Director," he says, "I always found him very easy to work with." Yet that isn't quite all he says. For he goes on to remark that

The Friends of the Kennedy Center
presents

THE KENNEDY CENTER PERFORMING ARTS SYMPOSIUM

Wednesday, April 5, 1978
12 Noon
American Film Institute Theatre

with

K E N N E T H   S A N F O R D

L E O N A R D   O S B O R N

of

D'OYLY CARTE OPERA

Our guests today are Kenneth Sanford, Principal
Bass-Baritone, and Leonard Osborn, Production
Director of the D'Oyly Carte Opera company.

Mr. Sanford has performed with D'Oyly Carte for
21 years. He has played Pooh-Bah in "The Mikado"
over 2,000 times, and adds to his record with his
performances here at the Kennedy Center. He will
also play Sentry in "Iolanthe" and King Hildebrand
in "Princess Ida."

Leonard Osborn joined D'Oyly Carte in 1937 as a
chorus member and understudy. After World War II
he returned to the company as a principal, retir-
ing in 1960. He was persuaded to re-join the
company in 1977 to stage the Jubilee production of
"Princess Ida" and remains as production director.

The D'Oyly Carte Opera company will perform in the
Opera House through April 29.

Our moderator today is Tony Riggs of WETA-FM, a long-
time Savoyard.

Note: The next Performing Arts Symposium, April 12,
will feature the American College Theatre Festival
with David Young, Rick Smith and Brooks Jones.

A guest appearance in America, 1978
(Well at least they spelt "Osborn" correctly)

"I do wonder if at times he pined for the days that had gone and craved to be a performer once again. It was very obvious at rehearsals, as the present incumbents performed his old roles, that he was re-living every note and step."

And those remarks are especially perceptive, and go some way towards explaining what became an increasingly unpalatable realisation for all concerned: that, taking everything together, the task he had set himself as Director was one in which he ultimately failed. He was in the right place – but at the wrong time. Had he taken the job on when he gave up performing, things might have turned out well. But the overriding feeling about him now was that he was too obviously rooted in the past, was too obviously trying to re-create the productions as they'd been in the 1950s.

But that was only one aspect of the problem, and probably the lesser aspect. For it was not only the productions that he was perceived as trying to drag back to the 1950s; he also gave the impression that he was trying to drag things back to how they'd previously been when it came to general attitudes to work and relationships; which was to say, the relationship between himself as Director on the one hand, and the rest of them – the performers he was directing – on the other.

The problem could be put like this. The 1950s was still a decade in which deference ruled – not to the extent it had ruled in pre-war decades, maybe, yet still to the extent that it was very much the norm. But during the 1960s and now in the 1970s a lot of that had changed. People were no longer so ready and willing to doff their caps to management, to accept Authority simply because it was Authority. And in his current role of Production Director, Leonard was as likely to have his authority questioned as any other authority figure in any other sphere of life.

Subconsciously at the very least, he had expected his authority to be unchallenged, just as it had been unchallenged when he was directing productions for amateur societies. He may well have assumed people would hang on to his every word, just as the amateurs had so patently hung on to it. It's possible to argue he was in this respect a poacher turned gamekeeper in that, when a performer himself, he had certainly not been afraid to question the dictates and decrees of Authority when he felt such questioning was justified – see, as the prime example of this, his letter to Bridget D'Oyly Carte on pages 57-8.

At a basic level, though, he had always accepted that Authority was Authority, whether it came in the form of his superior officers in the RAF, or Rupert and Bridget when it was the Cartes. Authority might not always do what he felt was right, but it was always to be respected. It's surely revealing that in two of his letters to the Cartes, he expressed the hope that the plans and arrangements about which he was writing in each case would receive their blessing (see pages 36 and 43).

But now when *his* authority was in any way challenged, he didn't really know how to react. No longer was having authority making him happy; and once again there surfaced those defences against insecurity - the impression of aloofness, of hauteur, the sharp put-downs, to which he'd been prone in earlier days. This is illustrated, for instance, by an anecdote that did the rounds regarding his attitude to rehearsals, as reported by one D'Oyly Carte follower of the time, Diana Burleigh:

> "He began rehearsals at ten o'clock. One of the chorus, who lived in Croydon, said he could either catch a train which would get him in an hour early, or one that would mean he arrived at rehearsals a few minutes late. The chap spoke to Royston Nash, who said 'Get the later train', so he duly did this, turning up puffing each time just after the rehearsal had started, and would always get a dirty look from Osborn, who totally disapproved."

"Unpunctuality, even slight, is in his eyes such a crime," as Cox sings in *Cox and Box*. Leonard's attitude was hardly unreasonable in itself. But giving a person dirty looks in public isn't necessarily the best way of getting that person to co-operate happily in what you want him to do. Nor does it encourage *other* people to co-operate happily either. Yet getting dirty looks may have been better than being ignored altogether, and Leonard at times gave the impression that certain members of the Company were "beyond redemption and not worthy of his assistance". And even if this was only an impression, impressions count. People sense these things and react accordingly.

Another relevant anecdote here comes from Michael Rayner, who had joined the Company in 1971. Rayner was engaged to play some of the light baritone roles: Captain Corcoran, Giuseppe and so on. But for Leonard's production of *Princess Ida*, instead of being cast in the equivalent part of Florian – he hadn't the figure to convince anyone he could have scaled the wall of Castle Adamant – he was shrewdly cast instead in the bass part of Arac. And at one rehearsal or performance he found himself being given not just a dirty look but a sharp reprimand:

> "When I was playing Arac, the sword that I carried was huge; about eight foot. I had to carry it wearing full armour, and at a certain point in the music just before 'We are Warriors three' I had to turn it upside down and thump it on to the stage.
>
> I did that and it hit a crack in the stage and went straight down. There was me in stage armour trying to get the bloody thing up.
>
> The producer was furious. "You did that on purpose," he said. "I saw you deliberately look for that crack."

The producer (unnamed in the published version of the anecdote) must have been Leonard. D'Oyly Carte were never again to do *Princess Ida* after the summer of 1978, and in any case Leonard was still producer when, the following year, Rayner left the Company. And the fact that Rayner claims Leonard was furious at what had happened rather than merely annoyed – or even, as he might have been, amused – suggests that relations between the two of them were not of the easiest.

Whether Rayner answered him back on that occasion, or whether he had a dig at his reaction in private, who's to say? But if he did have a dig at him for that or anything else, he wouldn't have been alone. At some point during his period as Director, Leonard acquired the nickname "Laddie Osborn" from the fact that he was still addressing the male choristers as "Laddie" just as he had done in the past. It wasn't a nickname used to his face; to his face he was always, in professional situations, "Mr Osborn". But it was a nickname used by a number of Company members of both sexes, and it wasn't a nickname used with particular affection.

Nicknames, admittedly, can be laughed off by most people without too much upset. Less easy to laugh off was something that was later to happen at a Company party. Two of those present allowed themselves to mimic him to the unashamed delight of the gathering as a whole. And this could have hurt, given especially that one of the two was Meston Reid, one of the then principal tenors who, by a somewhat unhappy chance, had been pictured with Leonard in a 1977 issue of the *Savoyard* cheerfully practising the *Ruddigore* hornpipe.

And *impossible* to laugh off was the fact that, after he had been Production Director for two and a half years or so, one or two of the performers had started ignoring some of the changes he was trying to initiate, pretty well telling him to mind his own business. And not only was this impossible to laugh off, it was obviously something that couldn't be allowed to continue.

Pointers to what was happening in this respect were bound eventually to come to the notice of the management, in particular Frederic Lloyd, and in due course they did. It's conceivable that Lloyd, never a person to go looking for trouble, may at first have turned a blind eye to the situation, hoping it would eventually resolve itself. But when it became clear that was not going to happen, even he had to act; and on January 10th 1979 he sent another of his private and confidential memos to Bridget:

"I am really very concerned about Mr Osborn as a producer" (*he wrote*). "I know that he has the right ideas and that he knows what should be done but, frankly, I do not think that he has the authority to get his point[s] over, and during the last two months I have come more and more reluctantly to the conclusion that he cannot really cope with the Company."

As proof of this he (Lloyd) penned another memo the same day reporting on what he regarded as over-playing that had become prevalent in Act Two of *The Pirates of Penzance*, a performance of which he had recently seen on tour. "I spoke to Mr Osborn about it, and I regret that it seems to me that nothing has been done," even though, he claimed, he doubted whether any action that Leonard might attempt to take to rectify the problem would be likely to have any effect. Parts of that act, he considered, had become "the height of vulgarity". The finale could "almost be described as 'The Laughing Policeman'. I fear," he concluded, "that Mr Osborn is not able to control it."

Yet things can't have been as bad as all that, for less than two months later he and Bridget were both writing to compliment him on his handling of that year's Sadler's Wells Last Night.

"Dear Mr Osborn (*this was Bridget*)
    I thought our Last Night was a very great success this year and was obviously much enjoyed by everyone.
    Certainly your influence has had an excellent effect, and thank you very much for all the hard work you must have done to make it so."

"My dear Leonard (*this was Lloyd – and note the "Leonard" again*)
    Just a line to thank you for all the effort you put into making the Last Night such an enormous success. I think all of us agree that it was a very well controlled evening, but enormous fun. Congratulations!"

And obviously congratulations from those quarters were not to be sniffed at. But how did the control Leonard exercised over the Last Night (assuming he did exercise it) tie in with his failure to exercise control at other times? The answer must surely be that Bridget and Lloyd were sending out mixed messages – messages, that is, suggestive of both firmness and lack of it - and that the performers were picking up those mixed messages whatever Leonard himself might be doing,

For though they – Lloyd especially - felt concern about what was happening, they shied away from doing anything about it; or at least they shied away from doing anything about it for several months. In May 1979 the Company were due to go off on their tour of Australia and New Zealand, an expedition that, from the point of view of their performances, overshadowed everything else that year – which meant it was not the time, unless it really became unavoidable, to start rocking the boat where the overseeing of those performances was concerned. It possibly helped in this respect that *Pirates*, whether still being over-played or otherwise, was not among the operas taken on the Australian tour.

Furthermore, and overshadowing things to a still greater extent, this was the time when the whole future of D'Oyly Carte seemed in the balance; when it had become questionable whether the Company had much of a future at all. There had been reports and talk of it being in difficulty – that is, financial difficulty – even before the Centenary season of 1975. Now the talk had moved on to encompass the disturbing possibility that it might have to close.

The result was, it wasn't till November – ten months after Lloyd's January memo and two months after the Australian tour had ended – that the question of Leonard and his inability to cope returned to the agenda. Was something going to be done about it at last? Or – the alternative couldn't be ruled out – was procrastinating still to be the order of the day?

Lloyd at least had no doubts. In his memo he had suggested that this should definitely be the time when something was done. Indeed he had indicated what, in his view, that something should be. "I think it is essential," he wrote, "to have a younger man on the production side of the staff … I think we must look for an energetic, courageous character who would be prepared to be a staff producer." Now in November, while in this instance giving Leonard a sort of pat on the back rather than saying anything further to his denigration, he emphasised the same point again:

> "There is no doubt that, though Mr Osborn is doing, and has done, a very good job, I am certain that the time has come for us to look around for a younger man who could perhaps come in for a year or so as his assistant."

And before long they found a candidate who fitted the bill. But meanwhile things had come to a head within the Company as a whole. Discontent was rife, especially with the way rehearsals were being conducted. In January 1980 the performers held a couple of meetings among themselves to discuss their complaints in this regard as well as other matters relating to the general running of things; and in the course of the second of those meetings they dropped a bombshell. A vote was taken – taken and carried - a vote of "No confidence in Leonard Osborn in his capacity as Director of Productions".

This vote of no confidence was passed to the management as the concluding paragraph of a closely typed two-page document drawn up in the wake of the meeting, a document that forcefully detailed their complaints and what they felt should be done about them. One of those complaints centred round Leonard's ideas about the delivery of dialogue. The Company felt, said the document, "that whilst the classic style of delivery is desirable in certain productions, it should be borne in mind that styles in more recent productions call for a more modern approach." Another complaint was the impression he gave of regarding certain performers as being beyond redemption.

But the most damaging complaint of all was a condemnation of the manner in which, at rehearsal after rehearsal, he and Jimmy Marsland behaved towards each other. Clearly the two of them didn't get on, and "everybody would like to see an end to the bickering and strife between Mr Osborn and Mr Marsland which is the predominant feature of virtually every joint production call at present," as it was cutting rehearsal time by half and destroying the concentration of everyone else – though they made it obvious they considered Leonard the greater culprit; Leonard, for whom punctuality, together with a previous dislike of time-wasting, had patently gone by the board.

In a full-length book about the D'Oyly Carte Company that I wrote some years ago, I stated that Leonard's spell as Production Director was regarded by many people as a disaster. It's a statement I've regretted ever since that book came out. What was I doing saying that one of my all-time favourites in the Company was a disaster, rubbishing his reputation in this way?

But the word "disaster", with all its connotations, was the word used when talking to me about him by someone close to the Company; and it's hard not to concede this was fair comment. To be the subject of a no confidence vote – especially in so tightly-knit a Company as D'Oyly Carte – what could be more damning? What, for someone like Leonard on whom D'Oyly Carte exerted such an emotional pull, could be more hurtful, more distressing?

(There was, though, a particular irony about the antagonism Jimmy Marsland and he developed towards one another. Back in 1974, in an interview in the *Savoyard*, Marsland had been asked to choose his top ten D'Oyly Carte performers – from among those, that is, he had personally known – and in his ten he had actually included Leonard, who he'd described as "an artist of great talent". He also, intriguingly, had included Margaret Mitchell – "a marvellous Phyllis. Her voice used to soar.")

Leaving Leonard's own feelings momentarily aside, though, the passing of that no confidence vote did have one positive outcome, namely that it led without any further delay to the changes that had by then become inevitable, and, in the process, cleared the air. On January 30th Frederic Lloyd wrote Bridget another memo, a memo written this time with an unconcealed feeling of relief. Nor was he the only person in the story who now felt relief:

> "I had a meeting with Mr Osborn this afternoon and explained to him the position, and told him that Mr Wilfred Judd was joining us as Associate Producer, and that I expected him to be responsible for general production, and that we wanted Mr Osborn, for the time being, to concentrate on dialogue and character work, and, frankly, Mr Osborn was heartily relieved.
>
> He accepted the suggestion almost gratefully, and I am under the impression that really he has been finding all the pressure too much for him."

But yet again it can't have been as bad as all that for, less than three weeks after this, Lloyd was once more writing to congratulate Leonard on the success of his latest Last Night:

> "I think the Last Night was terrific, and I very much appreciate all you did."

Leonard's contract expired at the end of the year's tour that summer, and whether or not at his own request, it wasn't renewed. Wilfred Judd, having joined the Company in the spring as Associate Director, now took over the full responsibilities of Production Director on his own account. And given Lloyd's original suggestion to Bridget that the new Associate Director might initially work for a year or so as Leonard's assistant, this was sooner than he (Judd) had presumably been expecting.

And so it was that one day at the beginning of August, after an association that had begun all but forty-three years earlier, Leonard made his exit from D'Oyly Carte for the third and final time.

"He Was Good, Wasn't He?",
1980-94

His final exit from D'Oyly Carte. The first time he'd left the Company it had been to join the RAF. The circumstances then meant that, emotionally, it had been a relatively easy departure, a departure forced on him by outside events and one that was in no way a reflection on him in any personal sense. The second time had been in 1959, when his departure was personal in every respect, and he had left feeling embittered and rejected. This latest time was surely, and even more graphically, a personal rejection too.

So did he feel embittered and rejected once again? The answer, according to Tony Osborn, was no. Rather it seems likely that at least part of him was not sorry to go – that he finally realised he'd had enough. His undisguised irritation with some of the other members of the Company, the bickering in which he'd allowed himself, totally uncharacteristically, to indulge, and the way he'd taken to truncating rehearsals, certainly suggested something of the kind.

He had been brought back into D'Oyly Carte, he came to believe, in the hope that he might revive the Company's fortunes and its artistic standing in the difficult years just past. If this was the case, he recognised he hadn't succeeded in the task, and, indeed, the Company was to close just eighteen months later. But he had tried. He had done his best. And the feeling one has done one's best in any situation can be a comfort – can even have its satisfying side – however unhappy and below expectations the result.

There was satisfaction in another sense as well. With any performer in any field of entertainment or other public endeavour, an addiction to the limelight can be, to a greater or lesser extent, what keeps that performer going. Once he has ceased performing, he (or she) can be plagued by an underlying sense of depression, a fear of no longer being wanted, no longer being loved. Leonard clearly had fears of this sort after 1959.

But in due course those fears had been dispelled, first by occasional contact with this or that branch of the Gilbert and Sullivan Society which had continued at least for a time; second by the warmth of his experiences with his three amateur producing societies; and third, most conclusively of all, by the way he was welcomed on his return to D'Oyly Carte. He may, as Production Director, have been re-living his own performances, but so with his return were any number of his former fans. He might be seventeen, eighteen, nineteen, twenty years older than he'd been when those fans had seen him last. But so were they.

In particular, as David Mackie recalls, middle-aged ladies at the stage door would ask in awed excitement "Is Mr Osborn there?" as though he was still the sprightly matinee idol they'd remembered from the past. True to form, he never let them down, responding to their eager approaches with "a gracious wave, a nod or a greeting" as circumstances required. Certain of those ladies, it's even been said, had only to hear his name to swoon and sigh "Leonard!" to remind them of their younger days. And if they hoped to see him on some particular occasion and then failed to do so, their reaction wasn't totally unlike that of star-struck teenagers.

"Oh dear, I have missed him again!" a journalist reported one of them saying sadly when she discovered he'd left the theatre after a performance at Sadler's Wells before she'd had a chance to get him in her sights. And each time something like that happened, it was living proof that in D'Oyly Carte circles he was not forgotten.

And now he had severed his connection with D'Oyly Carte and his D'Oyly Carte fans once more. Was this, so to speak, curtains? The answer here was "not exactly", for it was to be several more years before he severed his connection with the theatre altogether. Though nearly sixty-six – in other words, past the normal retirement age – he was still active, still wanted something to do.

But what? In November 1980 Frederic Lloyd enquired on his behalf whether an organisation called Knightsbridge Theatrical Productions currently had a vacancy of any kind that might suit him. And while that enquiry effectively led nowhere, another possibility had already been mooted that was ultimately to prove more fruitful: the possibility of his being found a position of some sort at the theatre in which he had played two memorable D'Oyly Carte seasons in the 1950s, the Savoy.

The idea of his becoming involved with the Savoy had first been floated back in 1962. At the end of that year feelers had been put out as to whether he'd be interested in becoming nothing less than its Manager at a time when the position of manager had become vacant. Now, though, it seemed that what was vacant were merely a couple of less exalted posts. One of these was clerical – "working on the credit cards" – and doing so "boxed up in a room and seeing no one", which hardly made the prospect sound enticing. The other was the Stage Door Keeper. Whether he took either of these lesser posts isn't clear; probably he didn't. But eventually the Manager's position became vacant once more; and this time, unlike the earlier time when he had reluctantly shied away from the idea, he went for the job and got it.

Or, at least, he got it on a somewhat *ad hoc* basis, initially becoming, as he described it, "a sort of odd job manager" who could be called upon at a moment's notice to run the front of house – and he was duly called upon in this way for a number of stints of varying lengths. In due course the post became full-time.

Leonard outside Sadler's Wells, 1980
(Photograph: Katie Barnes)

So there each night he would be, immaculate in evening dress, watching the audience coming in, smiling, welcoming them, though without being recognised by one person in a hundred. But every so often somebody who remembered him from his D'Oyly Carte days would show up, and then things would be very different. One person who showed up in this way was Melvyn Tarran, now well known for his extensive collection of G&S/D'Oyly Carte memorabilia and for the concerts and other G&S-based entertainments he presents at Sheffield Park in Sussex.

"I noticed him," Tarran movingly records of one night in September 1989 when the so-called "New D'Oyly Carte Company" was beginning its first Savoy season – "noticed him and wondered how he was feeling and what his thoughts were, he who but a few years before would have been mobbed by adoring fans.

'Hallo, Leonard,' I said. His face lit up. He was still 'not forgotten'."

Precisely when Leonard left the Savoy is also not clear. But leave it he eventually did. And if his advancing age had become one reason for this, another reason may have been the health of his wife.

Since they'd taken on the Purley Oaks shop in 1964, he and Eileen had gradually grown closer, and by now he had come fully to realise how much he loved and needed her. During the shop years she had many times been present, a quiet but happy figure, at his amateur productions, and had also been with him on those occasions when he'd gone to D'Oyly Carte as a member of the audience. And though when he'd eventually returned to the Company she had stuck to her determination not to accompany him on his *British* tours, she did go with him on the tours of America and Australia and New Zealand.

But then, early in the 1990s, she developed cancer. She was admitted to the Royal Marsden Hospital in Sutton, not far from their latest home, and there on October 29th 1992 she died. The cause of her death was given as "Non-Hodgkins Lymphoma". Her funeral took place at North-East Surrey Crematorium in nearby Morden. Leonard, distraught, was now on his own.

Tony Osborn, meanwhile, had been pursuing a successful career as a photographer in the publishing field. At the time of writing he is Ticketing Manager for Haymarket Exhibitions Ltd, while for about a couple of years his wife Caroline wrote for the *Gramophone* magazine. Martin Osborn, having gone to Australia, has remained there ever since, though he has returned to England for holidays and for other reasons from time to time – on five occasions with *his* wife Daphne whom he married in 1978.

Back, though, to Leonard himself. For a year and more after Eileen's death he continued to live somewhat wretchedly in the Sutton flat. A decision would now have to be made about his future, and taking that decision became, almost by default, the responsibility of Tony Osborn. Early in 1994, after looking into various options including, as a first thought, getting him into an RAF home, Tony managed to secure him a place in Denville Hall in Northwood near Pinner in Middlesex, a home for retired actors and, when there were vacancies, other people from the world of the theatre.

Denville Hall
(By permission of Denville Hall – photograph by Lisa Bowerman)

He went there first for a short holiday. But even as a resident he was to be there only about six months, six months moreover that included a spell in Northwood Hospital. The problem that necessitated hospital treatment was kidney trouble, and the hospital did what it could for him, insofar as the nature of his condition and his age permitted. The hospital stay, though, made him thoroughly miserable – made him glad to be back at Denville Hall – and Tony regretted not having got him into the Hall sooner. For there he was among people like himself, people who had had lives and experiences to which he could relate. There he felt settled. There he could be reasonably happy.

Or, at least, he managed to suggest he was happy there when he was in company. But there was certainly one occasion on which the mask slipped. He'd had a visit from David Mackie, the colleague who had formed a particular friendship with him in his later D'Oyly Carte days. And as the latter was leaving, he (Leonard) suddenly blurted out: "This growing old is bloody awful!"

Then, towards the latter part of that summer, 1994, as if kidney trouble and growing old in a general sense were not enough to cope with, there came the first signs of another potential cause of distress: senile dementia. But by now he was near the end. Sometime in the early autumn he caught broncho-pneumonia, and on September 28th, without recovering, he died. He was just six weeks away from his eightieth birthday. On his death certificate he was described as "Theatre Manager, Retired".

His funeral took place, as Eileen's had done, at North-East Surrey Crematorium. The date was October 12th. Martin came back from Australia to be there, as he had likewise come back for Eileen's. Both he and Tony were too upset to remember much about the occasion. Tony does remember a number of people from the Savoy Theatre being there, though of Leonard's erstwhile D'Oyly Carte colleagues the only one present was David Mackie. David remembers a fox suddenly appearing as they stood in the crematorium grounds.

One evening in 1958 or '59, the "group" of D'Oyly Carte enthusiasts I've mentioned earlier in this book were congregating outside a theatre after a Company performance of *Iolanthe*. It was the time of the craze for a Latin-American dance called the "cha-cha"; and when Leonard emerged from the stage door, one of the group mischievously suggested he insert a few cha-cha steps into the dancing trio in *Iolanthe's* second act next time the opera was played. Of course Leonard was never going to take this suggestion up. But he was highly amused by it, and happily signed all their programmes "Cha-Cha – Leonard Osborn".

Then a couple of nights ago, just before I wrote that last paragraph, I put on the recording of *Princess Ida* made during the Savoy season of 1954, and sat back letting that recording re-create in my mind Leonard's virile, exuberant and compulsively watchable performance as Cyril.

These are the ways in which I've always thought of him: as a genial, smiling figure surrounded by his fans, and a performer with an unfailingly exuberant and compulsively watchable presence on stage. And when I began work on this book I imagined I'd be writing a story in which smiles and exuberance were ever-present themes. I certainly wasn't expecting to write one featuring so much private and personal unhappiness, so many spats between himself and other people in D'Oyly Carte, and so many manifestations of insecurity and lack of self-confidence.

And yet ... doesn't all that make him a more interesting character than if he'd had no unhappiness, if he'd never experienced difficulties with other people, but had gone through life on a cloud of untroubled bliss and contentment? It may even be that the intense energy and concentration he put into his acting and singing was his way of keeping on an even keel, at least while he was on stage.

But whether this was so or not, it takes nothing from his brilliance as a performer, takes nothing from the pleasure and delight he gave to the vast number of people who made up his audiences over so many years. So let's leave him by repeating (more or less) the warm and admiring verdict on him given by Hugh Jones that I quoted in the first chapter:

"He was good, wasn't he?"

Leonard at the Stage Door, New Theatre, Oxford

147

Index

(Figures in bold type indicate illustrations)

151

Morden, 144
Morey, Cynthia, 63-4, 75, 84
Morgan, C. William [Billy], **34**, 90, 101
Morgan, Fisher, 61, 64, 76, **77**, 82, 87
Mornay, Joy, 4, 83

Nash, Royston, 131, 136
New Haven [USA], 52
New Moon, The, 115
New York, 17, 33, 35, 52-3, 81-2, 86, 108
Newby, Herbert, 50, 57-8, 63, 83, 104, **110**
Newcastle, 41
Nightingale, Alfred, 42-3, 57-8
North-East Surrey Crematorium, 144, 146
Northwood, 144, 146
Norwich, 17, 26, 30-1
Nottingham, 17, 41

Oldham, Derek, 2, 7, 26, 38, 122
Oliver, Vic, 55
Opera Club of Reigate and Redhill, 116, 118-20
Osborn, Anthony (son); see Osborn, Tony
Osborn, Caroline (daughter-in-law), 144
Osborn, Daphne (daughter-in-law), 144
Osborn, Eileen (wife), 20, 59, 86-7, 112, 114-15, 126, **127**, 128-9, 144, 146
Osborn, Frederick (brother), 9, **10**, 86, 114
Osborn, Frederick (father), 7, 9, **10**, 11-12
Osborn, Leonard
    accident in *Ruddigore*, 66, 68-9
    advertising work, 112, **113**
    affair with Margaret Mitchell, 46, 48, 55-6, 59, 69, 86-7
    amateur performances, 13, 115-16, **117**
    anniversary celebration, 93
    American tours, 17, 31-5, 48, 52-3, 57, 72, 81-3, 86, 88, 116, 130-1, 133, **134**, 144
    as Box, 7, 33, 44, 50, 53, 57-9
    as Cyril, 76, **77**, 78-9, 82, 84, 86, 96-7, 106, 146
    as Danilo, 115
    as Dauntless, 7, 36, 38, **39**, 40-2, 46, 51, 57, 60, 66, **67**, 68, 76, 82, 84, 86, 93, 98, 101, 106, 108
    as Defendant, 15, **16**, 17, 19, 23, 32, 35, 50-1, 53, 57-9, 84
    as Duke of Dunstable, 7, 23, 26, **36**, 57, 84, 93, **94**, 97, 101, 106, 108
    as Fairfax, 22-3, 26, **27**, 28, **29**, 36, 52, 56-7, 59, 63, 68, 73-4, 82, 84, 92, 95-6, 101, 106, 108, 110
    as First Yeoman, 15
    as Francesco, 15
    as Frederic, 50-1, 53, 56, 84

Osborn, Leonard (cont)
    as Leonard Meryll, 15
    as Luiz, 118
    as Marco, 22-3, **25**, 26, 28, 36, 44, 48, 51, 54, 56-7, 63, 65, 75, 84, 97-8
    as Nanki-Poo, 13, 22
    as Paul Fontaine, 115-16, **117**
    as Ralph Rackstraw, 32-3, 51-2
    as Tolloller, 4-5, 19, 22, 28, 32-3, 57, 74, 82, 84, **85**, 93, 101-2, 106, 108-9,
        110, 118
    at D'Oyly Carte performances, 122-3, 131, 144
    at stage door, **54**, 60, **87**, 96, 118, 142, **143**, 146, **147**
    auditions, 13, 22
    Australia/New Zealand tour, 130, 138, 144
    birth, 7, **8**, 9
    blackout, 93
    blood donor, **124**
    character and looks, general, 24, 26, 32-3, 46, 64-5, 118-20, 135-6, 146
    childhood, 9, **10**, 114
    cricket umpire, 83
    dancing, 40-1, 93, 98, 101, 106, 146
    death, 146
    directing amateur productions, 116, 118-20, 130, 135
    divorce, 86
    D'Oyly Carte broadcasts, 78-9
    D'Oyly Carte chorister, 2, 13-15, **17**, 19, 22, 33, 61
    D'Oyly Carte concerts, **34**, 44
    D'Oyly Carte Director of Productions, 2, 116, 125-6, 128-33, **134,** 135-40
    D'Oyly Carte Last Nights, 54, 73, 97-8, 122-3, 131-2, 138, 140
    D'Oyly Carte principal tenor, 2, 22-3, 28, 31-3, 35, 50, 63-4, 111
    fans, 24, 26, 33, 46, 53, 60, 96, 100-1, 108-10, 122-3, 142, 144, 146
    final D'Oyly Carte performances, 106, 108-10, 120
    Flight-Lieutenant, 20, **21**
    gives talks/entertainments, 70, **71**, 72, 93
    golfer, 31, 44, **54**, 83
    handwriting, 11, 32, 64, **71**, 118, 121
    home/private life, 4, 59-60, 87, 112, 114-16, 144
    in Denville Hall, 144, 146
    in *Mikado* film, 15
    joins D'Oyly Carte, 14
    leaves D'Oyly Carte, 19, 99-102, 104, 106, 140-1
    letters, 19, 31-2, 35-6, 40, 43, 56-9, 68, 70, **71**, 83, 90, 121-2, 135
    marriage, 20
    "no confidence" vote, 139
    not playing Hilarion, 15, 76, 79
    organiser, 43-4
    performances, general, 12-13, 20, 24, 28, 46, 51, 63-4, 112, 119, 146
    RAF service, general, 19-20, **21**, 23, 81, 111, 135, 141

Reid, Meston, 137
Reigate and Redhill; see Opera Club of Reigate and Redhill
Richards, Arthur, 87, 96
Roberts, Helen, 23-4, 28, 32
Robertson, Joan, 90-1, 123
Rogers, Houston, **39**, **67**, **77**, **80**
Rooke, Leonard, 13
Round, Thomas [Tom], 3, 23-4, 28, 30-2, **34**, 35-6, 48, **49**, 50-1, 61, 75-6, 78-9,
    92, 96, 102, 111, 115
Ruddigore,   6-7, 23, 30, 36-8, **39**, 40-1, 46, **47**, 50, 53, 57, 66, **67**, 69, 76, 78,
    81-2, 84, 89, 97-8, 106, 111, 116, 122, 137

Sadler's Wells Theatre, 6-7, 17, 31-2, 35, 41, 46, 72-4, 84, 92, 97, 102, 115,
    123, 126, **127**, 128, 131, 138, 142, **143**
San Francisco, 81-2
Sandford, Kenneth, 96, 98, 102, 104, **110**, 123, 132-3, **134**
Sansom, Mary, **110**
Savoy Hotel, 33, 86
Savoy Theatre, 5, 13, 53-7, 59, 73, 76, 78-9, 84, 95, 122-3, 142, 144, 146
Scala Theatre, 14-15, 115
Sheffield, Leo, 14
Sheffield Park, 144
Shoeburyness, 19
Sinden, Frederick, 4, 44, **49**, 55, 64-6, 69, 95, **96**, 102, **103**, 104, 109, 116, 120
Skitch, Jeffrey, 4, 40, 64-5, 78, **80**, 83, 96, 98, 123
Sladen, Victoria, 76, 79
Smith, H. Arnold, 42, 68
Smith, Margaret, **110**
"Snookie"; see Evans, Eleanor
Snowdin, Kenneth, 4, 9, 11, 33
Sorcerer, The, 23, 72, 116, 129
Southampton, 33, 81, 83,
Southsea, 18
Spewack, Bella, 35
Springfield [USA], 57
Stell, John Laidman, 93
Stephens, Jerome, **110**
Stoddart, John, 102, 104, **105**, 106, 111
Stratford-upon-Avon, 66, 69, 86, 88
Streatham Hill, 84, 99, 104
Styler, Alan, 44, **45**, 46, 51, 56, 60-1, 64-5, 76, 82, 93, **110**
Sullivan, Arthur, 40
Sunderland, 30
Sutton, 12, 128, 144

Tarran, Melvyn, **iv**, 4, **21**, **25**, **94**, 144
Theatre Royal, Drury Lane, 54